Michelle Wibowo's
showstopper
WEDDING CAKES

Michelle Wibowo's
showstopper
WEDDING CAKES

10 TUTORIALS FOR SCULPTING TRULY AMAZING CAKES

To my Michael and Mikyla who give purpose to my life.

First published in November 2014 by B. Dutton Publishing Limited, The Grange, Hones Business Park, Farnham, Surrey, GU9 8BB.

Copyright: Michelle Wibowo 2014

ISBN-13: 978-1-905113-50-7

All rights reserved.

Publisher: Beverley Dutton
Group Editor: Jennifer Kelly
Art Director/Designer: Sarah Ryan

Book publishing

Copy Editor: Frankie New
Senior Graphic Designer and Photography Stylist: Louise Pepé

Magazine publishing

Editor: Jenny Royle
Copy Editor: Adele Duthie
Senior Graphic Designer: Zena Deakin
PR and Advertising Manager: Natalie Bull

Photography: Andy Mays – Inspired Images
Props and venues: Inspired Weddings
Wallpaper supplied by wallpaperdirect.co.uk
Printed by 1010 Printing Ltd., China

IMPORTANT INFORMATION

The Author and Publisher have made every effort to ensure that the contents of this book will not cause harm or injury or pose any danger. Please note that some inedible items, such as floral wires, ribbon and cocktail sticks, have been used in the projects in this book. All such inedible items must be removed before the cakes are eaten. Similarly, any non-food-grade equipment and substances must not come into contact with any food that is to be eaten. Neither the Author nor the Publisher can be held responsible for errors or omissions and cannot accept liability for injury, damage or loss to persons or property, however it may arise, as a result of acting upon guidelines and information printed in this book.

ACKNOWLEDGEMENTS

I would like to thank my husband Michael who has always been there for me and made all the impossible, possible; my father, my in-laws and my sister Cindy for their endless support; my best friends Wolfgang and Emma who have always encouraged me to start writing my first book; and my long distance friend, Anita, who is always online to cheer me up and keep me awake whilst I'm doing late night projects.

I would also like to thank Squires Kitchen for supplying all the materials needed for this book, as well as Beverley, Jenny, Frankie, Sarah and all the staff who are always very helpful; and Andy Mays from Inspired Images for his brilliant photography.

INTRODUCTION

When I was a teenager I loved painting, sculpting and baking, so I was delighted to realise that I could combine all these skills to create edible art. Most people imagine a wedding cake to be either round or square and decorated with flowers or fruit, however, I see cake as an art form – just as a painter sees a blank canvas or a sculptor sees a block of clay. I can express myself through an edible work of art and I hope to be able inspire others to look at food in a more creative way.

I have carefully selected the projects in this book to cover a wide variety of different skills, such as cake carving, sugar modelling, texturing and airbrushing. From the initial design through to the finishing touches, I hope to guide you through all the steps for creating a 3D cake sculpture, sharing my tips and tricks along the way. What's more, as a professional cake maker I know how important practical aspects are, so I have made sure to include tips on how to store, serve and transport the cakes safely based on my own experiences.

If you already have some experience in cake decorating, I hope to be able to help you create your own professional-looking wedding cake sculptures. I use standard tin sizes for the cakes in this book, so they can be baked in a regular domestic oven and most of the equipment and ingredients can be easily found at your local cake decorating supplier and DIY store.

This book gives me a great opportunity to share the techniques I have learnt over the years, from starting out as a complete beginner in cake decorating to becoming a professional sugar artist. Hopefully I can inspire you to explore your own creativity and give you the confidence to create unique cake sculptures from your own kitchen.

CONTENTS

EQUIPMENT AND MATERIALS

EQUIPMENT

The equipment required to make the cakes in this book can be divided into seven categories. From start to finish, these are:

• Baking the cake;

• Cake structure and armatures;

• Carving and setting up a cake;

• Coating, sculpting and decorating;

• Colouring;

• Finishing touches;

• Packaging.

BAKING THE CAKE

1 Baking parchment

2 Cake tins

3 Electric stand mixer

4 Kitchen scales

5 Measuring spoons

6 Mixing bowls

7 Oven (not pictured)

8 Pastry brush

9 Scissors

10 Spatulas

CAKE STRUCTURES AND ARMATURES

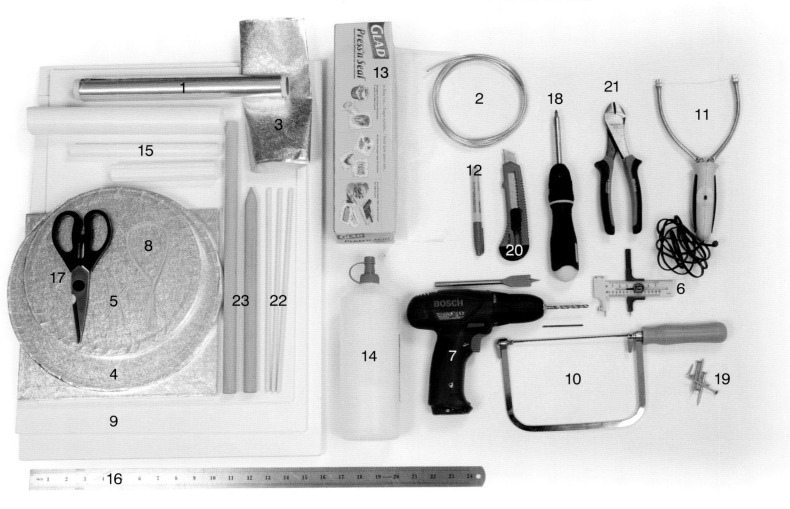

1	Aluminium foil	**13**	'Press and seal' food-grade plastic wrap
2	Aluminium craft wire	**14**	PVA craft glue
3	Cake board foil	**15**	PVC plastic tubes/pipes
4	Cake boards and drums	**16**	Ruler
5	Cocktail sticks	**17**	Scissors
6	Compass	**18**	Screwdriver
7	Drill with drill bits	**19**	Screws
8	Floral wires	**20**	Stanley knife
9	Foamboard	**21**	Wire cutters
10	Hacksaw	**22**	Plastic cake dowels
11	Hot-wire foam cutter	**23**	Large wooden dowels
12	Marker pen		

IMPORTANT NOTE

Remember that all inedible items used to make a cake must be approved for food contact and sterilised or covered in food-grade plastic wrap before they come into contact with any edible parts of the cake design, and must be safely removed before the cake is served. More advice about using cake armatures can be found on page 13.

CARVING AND SETTING UP A CAKE

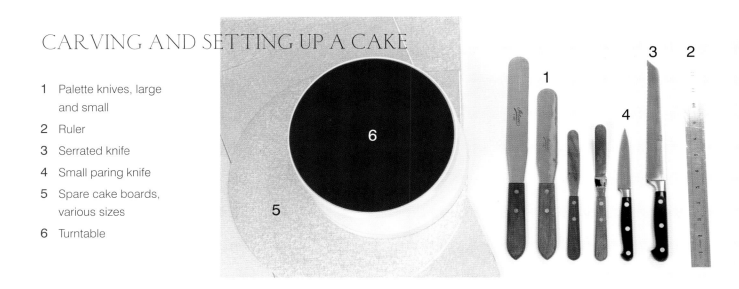

1. Palette knives, large and small
2. Ruler
3. Serrated knife
4. Small paring knife
5. Spare cake boards, various sizes
6. Turntable

COVERING, SCULPTING AND DECORATING

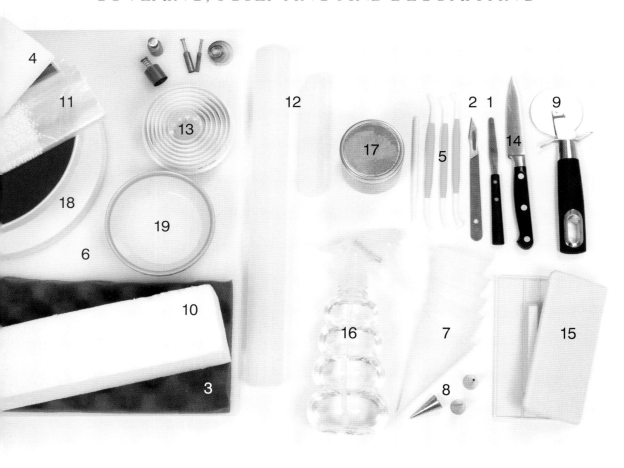

1. Blunt knife or Kemper tool
2. Craft knife
3. Food-grade dimpled foam
4. Kitchen towel
5. Modelling tools: Dresden tool, bone tool, cutting wheel, CelStick
6. Non-stick board
7. Piping bags
8. Piping nozzles (tubes): nos. 1, 2, 3
9. Pizza wheel
10. Polystyrene block
11. Re-sealable plastic food bags
12. Rolling pins, large and small
13. Round cutters, various sizes
14. Small paring knife
15. Smoothers
16. Spray bottle (made from food-grade plastic)
17. Sugar shaker for dusting
18. Turntable
19. Bowl of water

COLOURING

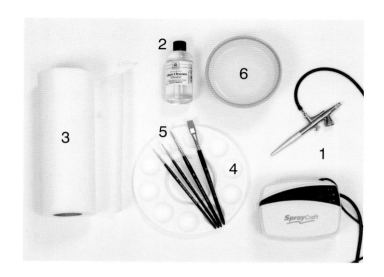

1 Airbrush set
2 Glaze cleaner (isopropyl alcohol) (SK)
3 Kitchen towel
4 Paint palette
5 Paintbrushes (various sizes)
6 Bowls of water

FINISHING TOUCHES

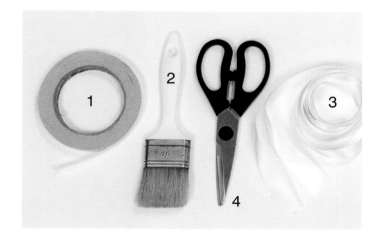

1 Double-sided tape
2 Dusting brushes
3 Ribbon
4 Scissors

PACKAGING

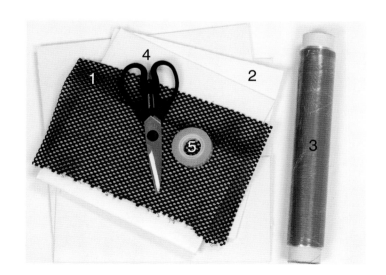

1 Anti-slip mat
2 Cake boxes
3 Cling film
4 Scissors
5 Sticky tape

MATERIALS

The edible materials that you need to decorate each cake will vary from project to project, but these essentials are used on almost every cake.

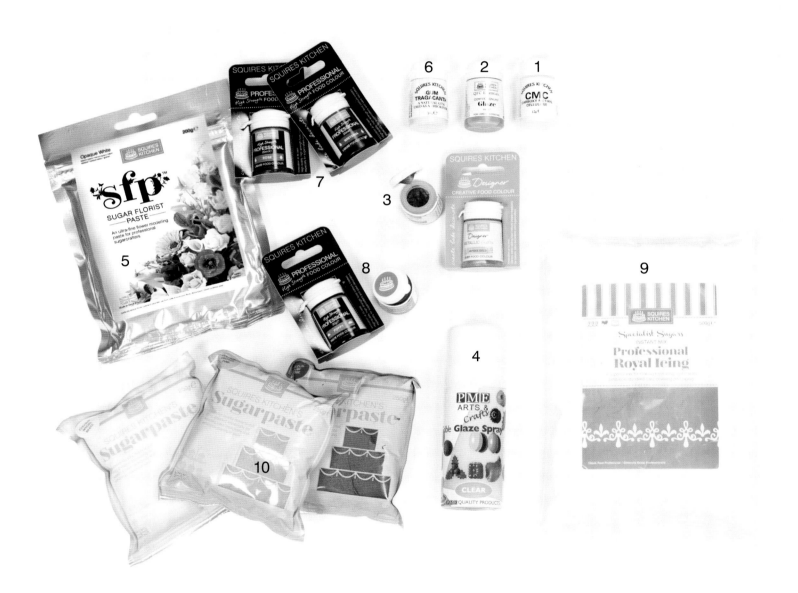

1   Cellulose gum (CMC) (SK)

2   Confectioners' glaze (SK)

3   Dust (powder) food colours (SK)

4   Edible glaze spray

5   Flower paste (SK)

6   Gum tragacanth (SK)

7   Liquid food colours (for airbrushing) (SK)

8   Paste food colours (SK)

9   Royal icing mix (SK)

10 Sugarpaste (rolled fondant) (SK)

RECIPES

Although the finished cakes in this book are quite elaborate, most start out as simple square sponge cakes which are then carved, assembled, covered and decorated. Square cakes are usually best for building cake sculptures; I would only use round cakes to create a ball-shaped cake or for a design with a rounded base. The cakes that I have used throughout the book can all be made with regular, domestic cake tins.

The standard portion size I use is approximately 2.5cm wide x 5cm long x 7.5cm deep (1" x 2" x 3"). When making a sculpted cake, always account for a few more portions than needed, as there will be some wastage as you carve.

SPONGE CAKE

The sponge cake I use is based on a Madeira cake recipe which I have modified to make it lighter, yet still firm enough to carve into a sculpted cake. I have also reduced the amount of sugar as the buttercream filling will provide extra sweetness. The recipe can be adapted to create different flavoured sponges, such as chocolate and lemon. The recipe chart below includes all the cake sizes that you will need to make the projects in this book.

1   Preheat the oven to 175°C/340°F/gas mark 4.

2   Grease and line the cake tin with baking parchment.

3   Cream the butter and sugar together until pale and fluffy, then gradually add the eggs to the mixture.

4   Sift the flour and fold it into the mixture carefully.

5   Pour the mixture into the tin and bake in the oven for the required time (see table).

6   To test if the cake is ready, a skewer inserted into the centre should come out clean. If you can see mixture on the skewer, return to the oven for a few minutes then test again.

7   Leave to cool in the tin.

	15cm (6") square	20.5cm (8") square	25.5cm (10") square	30.5cm (12") square
Butter (salted or unsalted)	225g (8oz)	400g (14oz)	625g (1lb 6oz)	900g (2lb)
Caster sugar	200g (7oz)	350g (12¼oz)	550g (1lb 3½oz)	800g (1lb 12oz)
Eggs, medium	3	6	9	12
Self-raising flour	225g (8oz)	400g (14oz)	625g (1lb 6oz)	900g (2lb)
For chocolate cake: add melted dark chocolate after flour	200g (7oz)	250g (8¾oz)	390g (13¾oz)	600g (1lb 5¼oz)
For lemon cake: add lemon zest with flour	1	2	3	4
Baking time	1–1¼ hours	1½–1¾ hours	1½–2 hours	2½–2¾ hours
Servings	18	32	50	72

Storage

Once the cake has cooled completely, leave the lining paper around it and wrap the cake in a few layers of cling film. It can then be frozen for up to two months.

BUTTERCREAM

Buttercream is normally used to fill and crumb-coat sponge cakes before covering them with sugarpaste. As most sculpted cakes have a large surface area, you will need to make up more buttercream than would usually be necessary for a standard cake. The recipe below makes 600g (1lb 5¼oz); multiples of this quantity are specified at the start of each project.

250g (8¾oz) unsalted butter, at room temperature

250g (8¾oz) icing sugar

100ml (3½fl oz) hot, pre-boiled water

Makes 600g (1lb 5¼oz) buttercream

1　Beat the butter until soft, then add the icing sugar and mix until pale and fluffy.

2　Add the hot, pre-boiled water gradually and continue beating until the mixture becomes fluffy again.

Flavour variations

Vanilla: add 1tsp of vanilla extract

Chocolate: add 150g (5¼oz) of melted dark chocolate

Lemon: add the juice and zest of 1 lemon

ROYAL ICING

I use royal icing on a lot of my cakes to stick pieces of sugar together, as well as to add decorative piping work. You can either use a ready-made icing such as SK Instant Mix Royal Icing or make your own following the recipe below.

8g (¼oz) dried albumen

300g (10½oz) icing sugar

50ml (1¾fl oz) cold, pre-boiled water

Makes 350g (12¼oz) royal icing

1　Mix the icing sugar and albumen together.

2　Add the water and beat until fluffy.

To adjust the consistency of royal icing, increase or reduce the amount of water added.

MODELLING PASTE

Sugarpaste alone is too soft for modelling, so I add ¼ teaspoon of CMC gum (also known as carboxymethyl cellulose or Tylo powder) to every handful of sugarpaste to make it firmer. By making your own modelling paste you can adjust the consistency by adding more or less CMC gum: the more you add, the firmer the paste will become. If you add too much, the paste will crack easily when you knead it; to resolve this you can always knead in more sugarpaste. Once the modelling paste is dry, you won't be able to knead it or adjust its consistency, so keep it sealed in a food-grade polythene bag whilst you are not using it.

You can also buy ready-made modelling paste, such as Squires Kitchen Mexican Modelling Paste (MMP), which will give the same consistency each time you use it.

CRISPED RICE CEREAL MIX

I use a mixture of crisped rice cereal and marshmallows to make bulky pieces on my models, as sugarpaste can be too heavy. The mix is soft and pliable when warm, so can be moulded into shape easily before it cools down and hardens.

100g (3½oz) crisped rice cereal

60g (2oz) marshmallows

15g (1tbsp) butter

Makes 160g (5½oz) crisped rice cereal mix

1　Melt the marshmallows and butter together in a microwave on a high setting for 1 minute.

2　Stir well and pour the crisped rice cereal into the mixture. Stir until well mixed.

TOP TIP

If the mix cools in the bowl you can always reheat it in a microwave to soften it again.

BASIC TECHNIQUES

CAKE SUPPORTS AND ARMATURES

What is a cake support?

A cake support is part of the structure between layers of cake that helps hold them in position. Cake supports, such as dowels, thin cake boards and pieces of foamboard, will help stop a large cake losing shape, or even collapsing. Any cake support that is used inside a cake must be made of materials approved for food contact or covered in food-grade wrap or foil.

What is an armature?

An armature is a rigid structure that helps hold the overall cake structure in place. These can be made from large wooden dowels, aluminium wire and lengths of PVC pipe. A cake taller than 10cm–12.5cm (4"–5") will need dowelling to support each layer of cake, but doesn't necessarily need a whole armature. Depending on the proportions of the cake, sometimes a design may be stable enough to remain upright with only cake supports. As with cake supports, armatures must be made of materials approved for food contact or covered in food-grade wrap or foil. Any small parts such as screws must be securely fixed to the armature before being covered completely in wrap or foil.

When does a cake need supports and armatures?

Most large, three-dimensional sculpted cakes and sugar sculptures will require both cake supports and armatures, but it is the density of the cake which determines how deep it can be before it starts to deform without them.

For example, a three tier cake with 20.5cm, 25.5cm and 30.5cm (8", 10" and 12") tiers that are 7.5cm (3") deep would need supporting cake boards and dowels but no armature. However, a three-tier cake with 15cm (6") deep tiers may need both cake supports and a central armature to hold it upright.

The recipes I use in this book give a standard serving size of approximately 7.5cm (3") deep or up to a maximum of 10cm (4") deep; this depth makes it easy to cut manageable-sized portions from each layer. Any cake deeper than 7.5cm–10cm (3"–4") will require dowelling to prevent it from collapsing (see page 18).

To create larger or bulkier parts of sugar sculptures or unusual shapes, I use crisped rice cereal mix (see opposite for the recipe), polystyrene dummies or aluminium foil. These materials are lighter than cake or sugarpaste so will not cause the cake to collapse. As my sugar figures are often caricatures, I make the head out of aluminium foil so I can create an exaggerated head shape that is light enough to sit on the sugar figure without it making it top-heavy, then cover it with modelling paste and decorate as normal.

Avoiding contamination

When you are using inedible supports and armatures in a cake, such as foamboards, wooden or plastic dowels, aluminium foil, plastic pipes, etc., it is important that these do not come into contact with the cake or any part that will be eaten. In order to make the cake safe to eat, it is important to follow these steps to avoid contaminating the cake:

• Always wrap all of the inedible parts in food-safe food sealing wrap or cake board foil so that they are unable to contaminate the cake.

• Always make the armature in a separate room away from where you'll be making the cake to ensure no inedible materials come into contact with foodstuff.

• Remember that any inedible parts, particularly those hidden inside cakes, may pose a choking hazard if they remain in the cake or come loose once the cake is cut. Before serving the cake, make sure that all inedible materials, such as plastic dowels, foamboards and figurines with foil or dowel supports, are safely removed.

• Always leave the main armature intact: do not try to dismantle it in case any inedible parts, such as screws or splinters, contaminate the cake.

• Never use an electric knife to cut into a cake containing inedible supports as you may cut through supports such as dowels and foamboard, causing them to break up and contaminate the cake. Remove dowels before cutting and cut carefully so as not to pierce through food sealing wrap or foil covering. Further instructions for serving cakes are given on page 21.

• If you will not be cutting the cake yourself, always inform the recipient that there are inedible items hidden inside the cake and instruct them how to remove them and cut the cake safely. Make sure they know which decorated parts cannot be eaten (e.g. figurines with internal supports or pastillage pieces which dry very hard). If you are leaving the cake with a wedding caterer, give them written instructions to avoid any confusion.

CAKE CARVING

Cake carving is a great way to create unusual shapes which cannot be made in a standard cake tin. Before you start to carve your own cake designs, you need to have a good idea of the proportions and details of the form you would like to create. If you don't prepare before you start, then you may encounter difficulties, such as carving away too much or making it out of proportion. Remember that it is always best to freeze a cake before you carve it, so it will hold its shape better as you carve. (Note that you can only freeze a cake once, so if you have frozen it straight after baking, you should not re-freeze it.)

Although carving a geometric shape may seem much easier than creating an organic, freehand shape, personally I think the opposite is true. It is quite challenging to create neat, accurate shapes when you are working with cake, which is soft and pliable. Creating an organic form is much more forgiving, as you can always build up the shape with off-cuts if you carve away too much.

Carving geometric shapes requires precision, especially if you're trying to replicate a building. You need to make sure that all the sides are completely straight, otherwise it will appear crooked. I recommend that when you are carving straight edges, use a cake smoother to help you achieve a sharp 90° angle.

LAYERING, FILLING AND CRUMB-COATING

Layering

To cut a small cake into layers, it is best to use a cake leveller which helps you cut it evenly and accurately. For larger cakes, use the technique below to help achieve even layers.

1 Level the surface of the cake with a serrated knife, removing the crusts from the top and bottom, then trim the sides straight. Removing the loose crusts will not only level the cake but will also help the sugarpaste stick to the cake.

2 Place the cake on a spare board and position it on a turntable.

3 Use the back of a long knife and a sterilised ruler to divide the sides of the cake into equal layers.

4 Hold a serrated knife horizontally and start cutting into the line, turning the cake as you go. Cut through the cake gradually and keep turning it until you reach the centre: try not to cut too deeply into the cake at first. Slide the first layer of cake onto a spare cake board.

5 Repeat steps 1–4 until you have cut the cake into even slices. For a 7.5cm (3") deep cake, cut the cake into four even layers.

Filling

When making a sculpted cake, make sure you don't use too much filling otherwise the layers are more likely to slide around as you carve.

1 Place the bottom layer of cake on a cake board and spread a thin layer of buttercream or jam over it with a large palette knife. I recommend using a 3mm–5mm (1/8"–1/4") layer of buttercream, or a 1mm–2mm (1/16") layer of jam so that the cake layers remain as stable as possible. Carefully place the next layer on top.

2 Repeat for the remaining layers and place the final layer on top to finish.

Crumb-coating

1 Once the cake is filled, trim the sides if necessary to make them straight and neat. This is particularly important if you are making a cake with precise, straight lines such as a building. Alternatively, carve the cake into the shape required following the project instructions.

2 Spread a thin layer of buttercream over the whole cake with a large palette knife. This seals in the crumbs and helps the sugarpaste coating stick to the cake.

3 Put the cake back in the fridge or freezer for about 30 minutes after you crumb-coat it, as this will allow the cake to firm up a little before you cover it with sugarpaste.

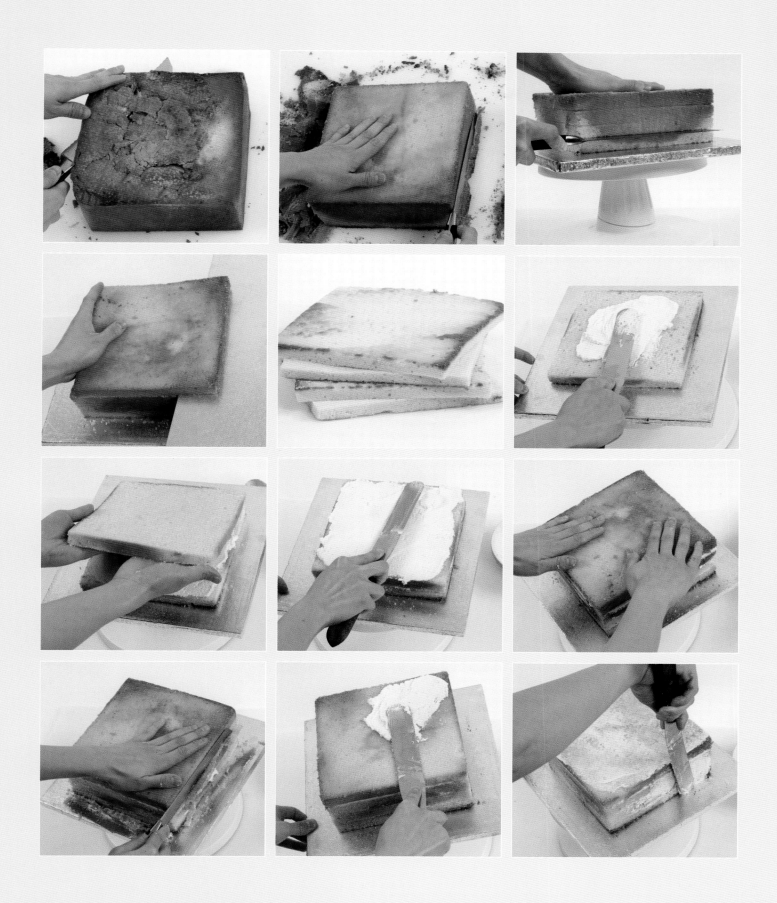

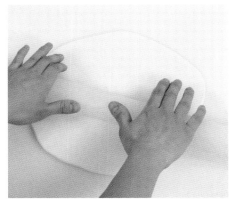

COVERING A CAKE BOARD WITH SUGARPASTE

I recommend that you cover the cake board with sugarpaste at least one day before you decorate the cake so that it is firm to the touch and won't mark easily.

All-in-one method

1   Roll out the sugarpaste to no thicker than 2mm (¹/₁₆").

2   Fold the paste over the rolling pin, lift it over the board and lay it in position. Gently roll over the paste with a rolling pin to expel any air bubbles.

3   Rub over the surface with a cake smoother to smooth it down.

4   Run a cake smoother at an angle around the edge of the board to create a tapered edge, if desired. Trim away any excess paste with a paring or palette knife.

5   Trim the board edge with ribbon (see right).

Fabric-effect method

1   Roll out some sugarpaste thinly on a non-stick board, making sure the paste is at least 2mm (¹/₁₆") thick.

2   Measure the size of the area you need to cover and cut it to approximately double this size. You may need to cover the drum in sections.

3   Using a pastry brush, dampen the cake drum with a little cooled, boiled water. Pick up the paste with your hands and arrange the sugarpaste loosely on the board to make loose folds.

4   Taper the edge of the board using a smoother if desired (see left) and trim away any excess sugarpaste with a palette knife.

5   Always trim the board edge with ribbon the same width as the board and in a coordinating colour. Use a non-toxic glue stick to hold the ribbon in place, taking care not to let the glue come into contact with any edible part of the cake. Overlap the join at the back of the cake.

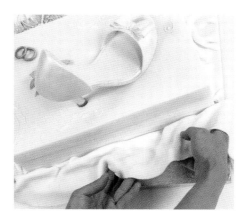

COVERING A CAKE WITH SUGARPASTE

All of the cakes in this book are covered with sugarpaste, also known as rolled fondant. Good kneading is the key to achieving a smooth, crack-free finish on your sugarpasted cakes: if you do not knead the paste enough, it may crack as you're coating the cake; over-kneading will lead to too many air bubbles and cracks in the paste, even before you roll it. Ideally, you should stop kneading as soon as you feel the paste coming together without any cracks.

How much sugarpaste?

When covering large or unusually shaped cakes, it is often difficult to know how much sugarpaste you will need. There is no easy formula to work it out, so I tend to do it by eye following the method that I have developed below.

1   Before you roll it out, take some sugarpaste and shape it roughly into the same 3-D shape and size as the cake.

2   Flatten the paste down with your palm or a rolling pin, then roll it out to approximately 2.5cm (1") thick. If, at this thickness, the paste is roughly the same shape and size as the cake you should have enough to cover it following either the all-in-one or section method described below.

3   For sculpted cakes, build up the shape of the cake with extra pieces of sugarpaste to create a more accurate shape before you cover it. The thickness of this extra paste means that it can be sculpted later, giving more detail to the finished piece.

All-in-one method

This is when you coat the entire cake (top and sides) with one piece of sugarpaste. This method is normally used for basic cake shapes, e.g. round or square. The bigger or deeper the cake, the thicker the sugarpaste will need to be, as it will stretch even more thinly over the sides of the cake. However, make sure the sugarpaste covering is no more than 15mm (5/8") thick.

1   Knead the required amount of sugarpaste on a non-stick board or work surface using a light dusting of icing sugar if needed. Start to roll it out from the centre, aiming to make it roughly the same shape as the cake. For example, if you're covering a round cake keep turning the paste while you're rolling it to ensure it is circular. Keep moving the paste as you roll it out to prevent it from sticking to the work surface and to minimise the amount of icing sugar you need as it can dry out the paste.

2   Fold the paste over the rolling pin, lift it and place it over the top of the cake. Starting from the centre of the cake, smooth over the surface with your hand or a smoother.

3   To create sharp edges on the covering, press two smoothers together at 90° around the top edge of the cake.

TOP TIP

The board can also be coated at the same time using the all-in-one method. If you have enough paste, carefully press the paste down into the bottom edge of the cake with a smoother and trim away any excess.

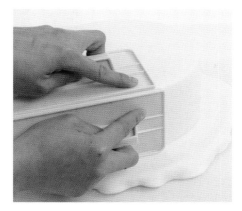

Section method

I recommend this method for large cakes, cakes over 15cm (6") deep, hard to reach areas, and for creating sharp edges on buildings.

1   Before you start to cover the cake, you need to work out how you will divide it into sections and how to conceal the joins in the paste. It is best to position the joins on the edge, bend, or pit of a cake, somewhere our eyes would expect to see a joint. If you can't hide the join completely, then make sure you find a place where it could be covered, either at the back of the cake, where there will be decorations to cover it, or where it will have a different texture.

2   Cut out pieces of sugarpaste to fit each section. Depending on the design, you can either use a template or carefully trim each section whilst holding the paste in position. To achieve sharp corners, cut a long strip of sugarpaste, attach it to the side of the cake and trim flush with the cake using a cranked palette knife to create a sharp edge. Repeat on the adjoining side and use smoothers to neaten the corner.

Double-sided method

This method is a more economical way of covering coloured cakes as you only have to use half the amount of coloured sugarpaste and it also means that you use less food colouring.

Measure the same amount of white and a coloured sugarpaste, place one on top of the other and roll out together. When rolling out the paste, be careful not to roll it so thinly that you can see the backing colour.

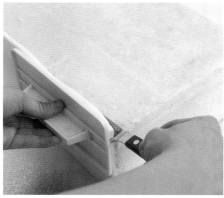

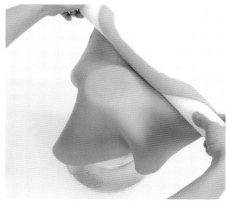

> ### TOP TIP
>
> The paste on the back can be white or any leftover coloured paste as it won't be seen.

DOWELLING A CAKE

Cakes that are particularly deep or tall may need dowelling to support the weight of the cake above. The number of dowels you need will depend on the size of the cake but always ensure that they are evenly spaced and fit within the size and shape of the tier above. Unless otherwise specified, use plastic dowels which are widely available from cake decorating suppliers (see page 152).

1   Wash the dowels in hot, soapy water then sterilise them by wiping them with clear alcohol. Allow to dry.

2   Mark where the dowels will be positioned (using a template if required) then push them down into the cake, ensuring they touch the board at the bottom.

3   Mark 1mm–2mm ($^1/_{16}$") above the top of the cake with a food colour pen, then remove the dowels and cut them all to size using wire cutters or a craft knife.

4   Re-insert the dowels into the cake then carefully place the upper tier on top.

SCULPTING

When sculpting, I tend to use a Dresden tool along with various sizes of paintbrushes. The Dresden tool with its two different-sized ends allows you to create different textures in sugarpaste easily, such as an elephant's wrinkled skin (see page 109) or teddy bear's fur (see page 69).

I like to use paintbrushes because I can use the handle for sculpting and the brush to dampen the sugar work as I go. Different sizes of brush lend themselves to different uses in sculpting. Only use paintbrushes with plastic (not painted) handles and sterilise them with clear alcohol to keep them clean.

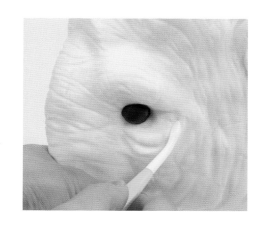

COLOURING

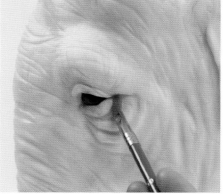

Painting

I tend to use paste food colours diluted with cooled, boiled water to paint directly onto sugar work. Fine, round paintbrushes are ideal for painting small details, such as facial features on sugar figures, and flat brushes are better for larger areas. For a lustre effect, dilute lustre dust food colours with confectioners' glaze and paint directly onto the cake. Remember to clean the paintbrush with glaze cleaner (IPA) after use to avoid spoiling the bristles.

Dusting

Dust food colours can create a softer graduation of colour and tone. It can be difficult to spray small, awkward areas with an airbrush, so it is preferable to use dust colours and a flat paintbrush. Lustre dusts can be used to add a soft sheen, but it is recommended that you brush SK Gildesol over the area before you apply the dust to help it adhere to the sugar.

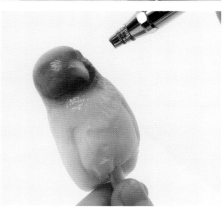

Airbrushing

There are many brands of airbrush available on the market at a range of prices. An airbrush from the cheaper end of the market may be perfectly adequate, but if you are looking to create lots of effects (and if you are making cakes on a regular basis) then I would recommend a professional airbrush. Airbrush colours are not always available in a wide colour range, so don't be afraid to mix them to achieve the correct colour. All Squires Kitchen's liquid food colours are suitable for use with airbrushes and I have used these throughout the book (see Suppliers, page 152).

Airbrushing techniques:

• The distance between the surface of the work and the airbrush affects the intensity of the colour. The nearer you are to the surface of the cake, the more concentrated the paint: move the airbrush closer to the cake when you want to paint a line.

• The pressure applied to the trigger controls the amount of paint and air coming out of the airbrush. Some airbrushes only have one lever to control both the air and paint flow: this is a good way to get used to using an airbrush if you're not familiar with one. Professional-quality airbrushes have one lever to control the airflow and paint flow separately, so you can achieve different effects once you've mastered the skill.

STORING CAKES

It is best to store finished cakes in a dry room that is approximately 18°C–22°C (64°F –72°F) in temperature and away from direct sunlight. I do not recommend that you store the cakes in the fridge, especially if you've used airbrush colours, as the colours will run when you remove the cake due to the change in temperature. Once the cake is cut, any leftovers can be kept in the fridge or, if kept in a freezer, you can extend their shelf life by up to three months. Remember that cakes can only be frozen once, so can't be put back in the freezer if they have already been frozen after baking.

The sponge cakes and buttercream I use in this book have a shelf life of approximately two weeks when stored correctly, so if you spend one week decorating the cake, it has another week's shelf life at room temperature, or up to two weeks in the fridge. I would not recommend using fresh cream or other fresh ingredients for a highly decorated cake as they have a much shorter shelf life and must be kept in the fridge.

Before you start making a cake, make sure you have a cake box where you can store the cake during and after decoration. Place a piece of non-slip mat under the base board to prevent the cake from moving around in the box and always use a well-fitting lid to protect the cake.

Cake boxes are ideal for keeping cakes safe, particularly if the cake is to be transported to the venue – these are available from cake decorating suppliers (see page 152). To transport a tall cake as seen in the picture, I stand two additional rectangular boxes (and lids) on their sides and slot them around the outside of the main cake box for extra height. Make sure the length of the box is at least 2.5cm (1") bigger than the height of the cake.

TRANSPORTING

If you need to transport the cake to a venue, it is preferable to travel by car as large, fragile boxes can be tricky on public transport! It is important to factor in your mode of transport when designing the cake to ensure that you are able to transport it securely. Always put the cake in a lidded cake box and place on a level surface, such as in the car boot, preferably with an anti-slip mat underneath it to prevent the cake from sliding around while in transit. Never put the cake on the car seat or your lap as there is a risk, especially for tall cakes, that they will fall over.

SETTING UP AND SERVING

Make sure the venue where the cake will be displayed has adequate storage and that there is a suitable display table for the cake. Make sure the floor is even so the cake won't wobble (particularly in wedding marquees) and check that there are no heat sources nearby such as a radiator, open fire or direct sunlight coming through a window. It is also a good idea to position the cake where there won't be passing traffic to minimise the risk of it getting damaged.

Although it is usually more difficult to cut and serve sculpted cakes, it is much easier if you follow a cutting guide. I normally make a diagram of the cake armatures as part of the cake (see the diagrams on pages 126–142). The diagram can also be colour-coded to make it easier to see which part is safe to cut.

The standard portion size I use for wedding cakes is approximately 2.5cm wide x 5cm long x 7.5cm deep (1" x 2" x 3"). Whatever the shape of the cake, it is simpler to cut each layer into grids based on the standard portion size. Each portion doesn't have to be exact, as long as they look more or less the same size.

TOP TIPS

Take a cake repair kit with you when delivering to a venue, just in case there are any mishaps on the way! A small bag of royal icing, a Dresden tool, edible glue and a paintbrush are all useful for fixing pieces that may have broken off or come loose.

When you make a sculpted cake, always bake a bigger cake than the amount of servings you need as you will lose cake as you carve (see page 11).

Projects

CLASSIC CAR

If you want to arrive at the church in style, a beautiful classic car is always a popular choice. Great for car enthusiasts and fans of everything vintage, you can now replicate the elegance of a classic car in cake. This cake is ideal for a small wedding, but you can make a larger version for more servings or present the car on a rectangular cutting cake.

Size: approx. 45.5cm x 15cm x 11.5cm (18" x 6" x 4½") | Serves 50

EDIBLES

30.5cm (12") square sponge cake

2 quantities of buttercream (see page 12)

SK Sugarpaste (rolled fondant): 500g (1lb 1¾oz) Bridal White, 500g (1lb 1¾oz) Tuxedo Black, 500g (1lb 1¾oz) Vintage Ivory

Modelling paste (sugarpaste + CMC, see page 12): 100g (3½oz) Bridal White, 250g (8¾oz) Tuxedo Black

SK Sugar Florist Paste (SFP, gum paste): 100g (3½oz) White

200g (7oz) SK Instant Mix Royal Icing

SK Professional Paste Food Colours: Jet Black, Poinsettia (Christmas red), Sunflower

SK Designer Metallic Lustre Dust Food Colour: Light Silver

SK Quality Food Colour (QFC) Dust: Pearl

SK Confectioners' Glaze

SK Professional Food Colour Pen: Black (optional)

EQUIPMENT

Basic equipment (see pages 6–9)

51cm x 20.5cm (20" x 8") piece of 10mm (³/₈") thick foamboard

35.5cm x 61cm (14" x 24") rectangular cake drum (board)

32-gauge floral wires: white

Round cutters: 3.7cm, 5.8cm, 7.8cm (1½", 2³/₈", 3¹/₁₆")

Round plunger cutter set (PME)

Piping nozzle: no. 1

Fine paintbrush (SK)

Flat dusting brush (SK)

Satin ribbons: 40.5cm (16") x 7mm (³/₈") width ivory, 2m (79") x 15mm (⁵/₈") width white

Templates and diagram (see pages 126–127)

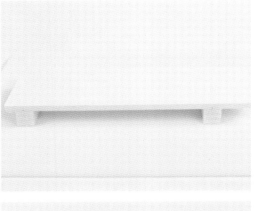

ARMATURES

1 Use a photocopier to enlarge the car templates by 200% and print out each template.

2 Use the car armature diagram to cut out the armature from a piece of foamboard using a Stanley knife. Following the diagram on page 126, assemble the support using craft glue and cover completely with food sealing wrap.

3 Roll out some Tuxedo Black sugarpaste to 2mm (¹⁄₁₆") thick. Dampen the underside of the armature with a little pre-boiled water and cover it with the paste. Leave to dry.

TOP TIP

Make the decorative pieces in advance to allow for drying time.

WHEELS

4 Roll out 250g (8¾oz) of black modelling paste to approximately 8mm (³⁄₈") thick. Cut out four circles using the 7.8cm (3¹⁄₁₆") round cutter for the tyres. Use a 5.8cm (2¼") round cutter to mark the inner edge of each tyre.

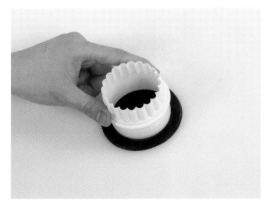

5 Roll out some ivory modelling paste to approximately 2mm (¹⁄₁₆") thick and cut out four circles with the 5.8cm (2³⁄₈") round cutter.

6 To make the hubcaps, stick each ivory circle in the centre of the black circles with a little cooled, boiled water. Mark a circle inside the hubcap with a 3.7cm (1½") cutter, then make a small circle in the centre with a 1.2cm (³⁄₈") round plunger cutter.

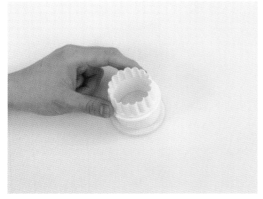

7 Roll out a small amount of ivory modelling paste to 1mm (¹⁄₁₆") thick and cut out four small circles using the 1cm (³⁄₈")

plunger cutter. Stick a circle in the centre of each hubcap. Use a small palette knife to mark the tyre tread around the edge of the tyre, then leave to dry.

8 Dilute some Light Silver lustre dust with a little confectioners' glaze, then use the mixture and a fine paintbrush to paint the hubcap and the circle around it. Once you have finished, clean your brush in glaze cleaner to prevent damage to the bristles and leave the wheel to dry.

TOP TIP

When surface painting with lustre dusts, it is preferable to mix the dusts with confectioners' glaze rather than clear alcohol. This will mean the colour stays on the cake and won't brush off easily after the alcohol has evaporated.

HEADLIGHTS AND WING MIRRORS

9 Following the step picture below, roll 2cm (¾") balls of ivory modelling paste and shape them into rounded cone shapes that are 2cm (¾") tall. Flatten the bottom of each cone against the work surface: this will be the front of the headlight. Insert a cocktail stick into the side of each cone to make a support for the headlight.

10 Roll out some White SFP very thinly, cut out two strips that are approximately 2mm (¹⁄₁₆") wide and attach them around the front of each headlight to make the rims.

11 Make another smaller set for the wing mirrors in the same way using 5mm (¼") balls, but do not insert cocktail sticks into them. Leave to dry on a spare board.

12 Once they are dry, paint the casing and the cocktail sticks with the Light Silver lustre dust mixture and paint the front of the light with some Sunflower paste food colour diluted with a little cooled, boiled water.

BRAKE LIGHTS

13 Roll out some White SFP very thinly and cut out a pair of rectangles that are each 5mm x 1cm (¼" x ³⁄₈") in size. Cut out two more rectangles that are approximately 1mm (¹⁄₁₆") larger than the first pair. Stick the smaller ones on top with a little cooled, boiled water and allow them to dry.

14 Paint the smaller rectangles with Poinsettia paste food colour and the trim with the diluted Light Silver lustre dust mixture.

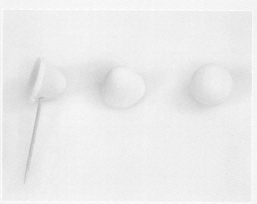

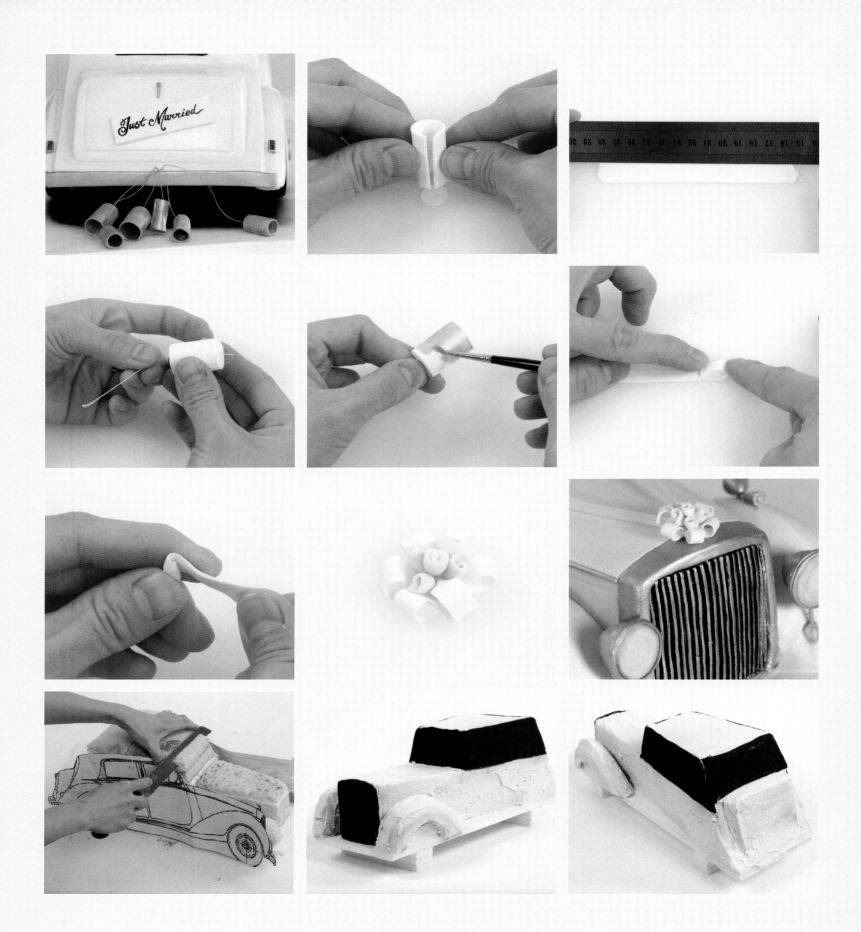

'JUST MARRIED' SIGN

15 Roll out some White SFP to approximately 1mm (¹/₁₆") thick, dust a spare cake board with icing sugar and transfer the paste to the board. Cut out a rectangle of paste measuring approximately 2cm x 8cm (¾" x 3³/₈") and leave it to dry.

16 Write the words 'Just Married' on the paste with either a Black food colour pen, or if you are more confident, use Jet Black paste food colour and a fine paintbrush.

TRAIL OF CANS

17 Roll out a small amount of White SFP very thinly. Cut out several different-sized circles from the paste using the small, round plunger cutters. Prick a hole in the centre of each circle with a floral wire and leave to dry on a spare board.

18 Use a pizza cutter and a ruler to cut out several 2cm (¾") wide strips from White SFP. Mark three or four lines along the middle of each strip with a clean ruler. To create the can shape, wrap the strips around the plunger cutters, then trim the paste to size. Remove the cutter, then stick the edges of the paste together with the round base using a little cooled, boiled water. Make as many as you wish, then leave them to dry.

19 Cut several 32-gauge floral wires to various lengths so that you have one for each of the cans. Bend one end of each wire into a hook and insert the other end through the hole from the can opening. Paint all the cans with the diluted Light Silver lustre dust mixture and allow the paint to dry.

FLOWER BOUQUET

20 Roll out some White SFP very thinly and cut out six 5mm (¼") wide strips. Bring the ends of each strip together to make a loop that is approximately 1.5cm (½") long. Arrange the loops together in a circle.

21 Cut out five thin, rectangular strips from some ivory-coloured SFP. Roll one strip of paste up tightly from one end to create a basic rolled rose shape. Make five rolled roses in the same way, arrange them in the middle of the loops and secure with a little cooled, boiled water. Leave them to dry before painting.

22 Once dry, dilute some Pearl lustre dust in a little cooled, boiled water and use a fine paintbrush to paint the loops and roses.

CAKE AND DRUM

23 Cover the cake drum with Bridal White sugarpaste and leave to dry (see page 16).

24 Layer and fill the 30.5cm (12") square cake with buttercream. Place the overhead template on the cake and cut it into sections using a serrated knife.

25 Spread a thin layer of buttercream over the top of the foamboard armature then place the pieces of cake on it in the correct positions, following the template as a guide.

26 Stick the side profile templates onto each side of the cake with a little buttercream. Use a serrated knife to carve the cake into shape following the outline of the template. Once you are happy with the shape, crumb-coat the cake.

27 Roll out some Tuxedo Black sugarpaste to approximately 3mm (¹/₈") thick then cover the areas for the windows with the paste.

28 Roll out a small, thin rectangle of black modelling paste, then use a clean ruler to emboss straight, vertical lines across the whole piece of paste. Use a paring knife to cut the bottom of the paste straight, stick the paste to the very front of the car for the grill and cut to size.

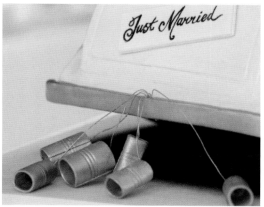

29 Roll out 500g (1lb 1¾oz) of Vintage Ivory sugarpaste to 5mm (¼") thick and cut out two strips that are 20cm x 50cm (8" x 19") in size. Use a little cooled, boiled water to stick each strip around each side of the cake to cover the bottom half of the car. Mark a line around the bottom half with a ruler before trimming away any excess paste with a craft knife.

30 Roll out 1kg (2lb 3¼oz) of Bridal White sugarpaste to 5mm (¼") thick then cover the whole car using the technique on page 18 to achieve sharp edges.

31 Use a craft knife to cut out the wheel arches. Mark the halfway line around the car with a ruler as before and cut along the line with a craft knife. Carefully peel back the white paste to expose the Vintage Ivory paste underneath.

32 Using the side templates for reference, mark on the outline of the windows and the front grill with a Dresden tool. Cut just inside the outline with a craft knife, being careful to only cut through the white sugarpaste layer, then gently peel back the white paste to reveal the black paste underneath.

33 Use the template and a Dresden tool to mark out the rest of the details on the sugarpaste covering.

FINISHING TOUCHES

34 Use a little royal icing on the back of each wheel to stick them to the armature inside the wheel arches.

35 Using the overhead template as a guide, attach the headlights and the wing mirrors to the front of the cake using royal icing.

36 Use the same template to position the brake lights and stick them in place using royal icing.

37 Brush a little royal icing over the back of the 'Just Married' sign and stick it to the boot of the car, taking care not to smudge the writing.

38 Take the cans made earlier, arrange the wires together to create a trail of cans, then attach each wire to the armature underneath the very back of the car with royal icing.

39 For the bumpers, roll out some White SFP very thinly and cut out two long strips that are approximately 1cm (³/₈") wide. Use the template to cut each bumper to the appropriate length, then stick them around the edge of the armature at either end of the car with a little royal icing.

40 Roll out four very thin sausages of White SFP to make the brackets then stick them to either side of the bumpers using a little cooled, boiled water and trim to size.

41 Use soft-peak consistency royal icing and a no. 1 nozzle to pipe on the door handles and the handle for the boot. Leave to dry.

42 Paint over the car's trim, grill, door handles and bumpers with the diluted Light Silver lustre dust mixture and a fine paintbrush.

43 For a glossy finish, paint the whole car with confectioners' glaze using a flat dusting brush.

44 Cut two pieces of ivory ribbon to approximately 18cm (7³/₁₆") long. Tuck one end of each ribbon into the window frame using a craft knife, then bring the other ends together so they meet at the front of the car and stick them in place with royal icing.

45 Use a little royal icing to attach the flower bouquet where the two ribbons join together.

Classic Car

ON THE WINGS OF LOVE

If the happy couple is jetting off to somewhere exotic for their wedding
or honeymoon, this is the perfect cake to celebrate the big day.
Remember that you can personalise the bride and groom's features to
make your sugar models look just like the newlyweds!

Size: approx. 45.5cm x 15cm x 10cm (18" x 6" x 4") | Serves 80

EDIBLES

20.5cm and 30.5cm (8" and 12") square cakes

2 quantities of buttercream (see page 12)

SK Sugarpaste (rolled fondant): 3kg (6lb 9¾oz)
Bridal White, 200g (7oz) Lullaby Blue

Modelling paste (sugarpaste + CMC, see
page XXX): 200g (7oz) Bridal White, 200g (7oz)
Tuxedo Black

500g (1lb 1¾oz) SK Instant Mix Royal Icing

SK Professional Paste Food Colours: Bluebell
(navy blue), Bulrush (dark brown), Chestnut
(soft beige), Edelweiss (white), Jet Black,
Marigold (tangerine), Rose

SK Professional Liquid Food Colours (for
airbrushing): Bluebell (navy blue), Edelweiss
(white)

Edible glaze spray (PME)

SK Professional Food Colour Pen: Brown
(optional)

EQUIPMENT

Basic equipment (see pages 6–9)

76cm x 51cm (30" x 20") piece of 10mm (³/₈")
thick foamboard

51cm (20") square cake drum

Wooden barbecue skewers

Fine paintbrushes: nos. 00, 2 (SK)

Satin ribbon: 2.05m (81") x 15mm (⁵/₈")
width ivory

Templates and diagram (see page 128)

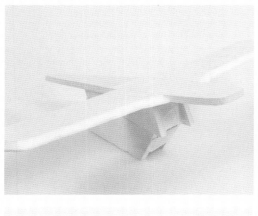

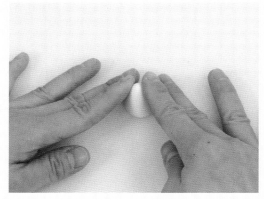

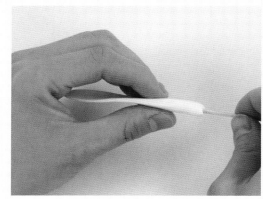

ARMATURES

1 Use a photocopier to enlarge the aeroplane and stand templates by 300%. Place each template onto a piece of 10mm (³/₈") foamboard and cut around it with a Stanley knife. Chamfer the edges of each wing then cover completely with food sealing wrap.

2 Assemble the pieces of the aeroplane stand following the diagram on page 128 and glue them together with craft glue. Attach the top of the stand to the bottom of the aeroplane base board with craft glue and completely cover with food sealing wrap.

WINGS

3 Roll out some Bridal White sugarpaste to 2mm (¹/₁₆") thick so that it is large enough to cover the underside of the wings. Dampen the base of the wings with a little

cooled, boiled water and cover with the paste. Trim away any excess paste with a sharp knife and leave to dry for 24 hours.

4 Roll out some white modelling paste to 4mm (³/₁₆") thick, place the tail wing template on the paste and cut out three tail wings with a cutting wheel. Insert cocktail sticks into the base of each tail wing: the stick will be inserted into the cake to provide support. Lay them flat on a spare cake board for at least 24 hours to dry. Turn them over halfway through the drying time to allow both sides to dry.

PROPELLERS

5 Roll a 2cm (¾") diameter ball of white modelling paste and taper one end into a cone shape: this will make the nose cone for the plane. Insert a cocktail stick into the flat bottom of the cone and stand it in a block of polystyrene to dry.

6 Roll a thin sausage of White SFP and cut it in half to make two sausages that are each 7.5cm (3") long. Flatten one half of each sausage with a cake smoother, then cut around the flattened edge with a cutting wheel to make a paddle shape. Insert a cocktail stick into the thicker end, twist the flatter end of the paste a little and leave to dry. Repeat for the second propeller blade. Secure the propeller blades to the nose cone with a dab of royal icing and leave to dry in a block of polystyrene.

7 Use Bulrush paste food colour and a paintbrush to paint the nose cone brown then add two brown stripes across the width of each propeller blade.

BRIDE'S UPPER BODY

8 Colour some white modelling paste with Chestnut paste food colour to make the

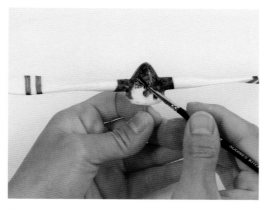

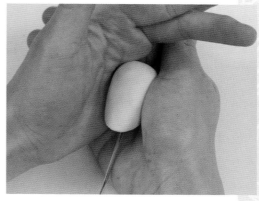
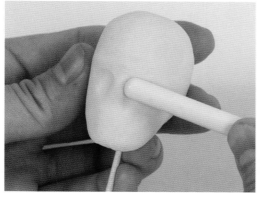
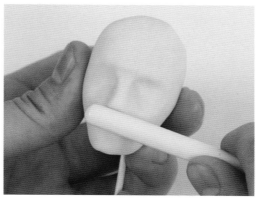

skin colour and leave in a sealed, food-grade polythene bag to develop for a day before use.

9   For the head, scrunch up some kitchen foil and manipulate it into a basic head shape. If the head looks too big then scrunch up the foil more tightly; add more foil if it looks too small. Make the head armature approximately 4cm (1½") tall.

10   Roll out a thin layer of the skin-coloured modelling paste, wrap it around the

armature so that the foil is completely covered and fill any holes in the foil with paste to prevent air bubbles. This layer will provide a smooth base and will help the paste adhere to the armature. Brush the surface with a little cooled, boiled water and cover the head with a thicker layer of modelling paste. Insert a cocktail stick into the bottom of the head.

11   Press the wider end of a CelStick into the face to make the eye sockets and bring out the nose. Mark the lip line with a Dresden tool and press it around the mouth to bring out the lips. To create a smile, make a small gap between the lips and add lines on either side of the mouth with a Dresden tool. Use the pointed end of a small CelStick, or a cocktail stick, to make the nostrils.

12   For the eyes, mark oval shapes in the paste with a Dresden tool or a small CelStick and mark a line above them for the eyelid. Leave to dry in a block of polystyrene.

TOP TIP

Being right-handed I find it easier to turn the head upside down to sculpt the right eye, so that it accurately matches the left one.

13   To add detail to the eyes, paint them with Edelweiss paste food colour to create a base colour. Paint a circle of Bluebell paste food colour in the middle of each eye for the iris and paint a slightly darker shade around the edge to add depth. Paint a small dot of Jet Black in the centre of each eye to make the pupil. Shade the eyelid with Bluebell diluted with some clear alcohol and paint along the eye line with Jet Black paste food colour. Paint the lower eye line in a slightly lighter shade than the upper eye line. Paint on the eyebrows with Chestnut paste food colour.

TOP TIP

The jaw line and brow bone are the main differences between a male and female face: to create a female face, make the jaw line softer and the brow bone less pronounced.

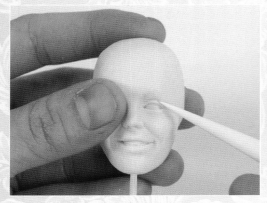
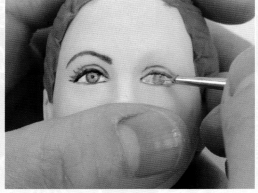
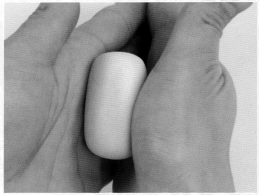
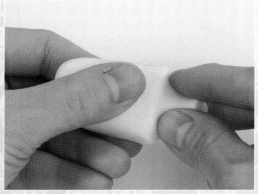
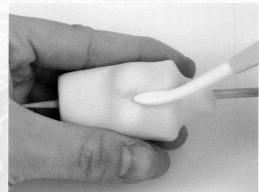

14 Add shading to the deeper areas of the face such as the corners of the mouth, nostrils and inside of the ears with Chestnut paste food colour. Paint the lips with Rose paste food colour, making the upper lip slightly darker than the lower lip.

15 To make the upper torso, roll a thick sausage of skin-coloured modelling paste that is approximately 2.5cm (1") in diameter and 5cm (2") long. Flatten the sausage between your hands, then pinch one end of the sausage to bring out the neck. Insert a wooden barbecue skewer all the way up through the neck. Roll a CelStick up the front of the body, pushing the paste up towards the top of the torso. Use a Dresden tool to mark on the cleavage line, then leave the torso to dry in a block of polystyrene.

16 For the hair, colour some white modelling paste with Bulrush paste food colour. Roll the paste into a ball that is approximately 1cm (³⁄₈") in diameter, then

flatten it down and stick it over the head with a little cooled, boiled water. Continue to flatten out the paste with your fingers until the scalp is covered. Roll a small ball of paste and stick it to the crown of the head for the bun. Use a Dresden tool to mark hair lines over the paste. To add curls at the front, roll tiny sausages of Bulrush-coloured paste and twist them with your fingers. Stick them to the front of the head using a little cooled, boiled water.

17 Remove the cocktail stick from the base of the head, then carefully push the head onto the skewer protruding from the upper torso. Roll out some white modelling paste thinly so it is big enough to cover the front and back of the torso. Trim one side straight using a cutting wheel. Use a little cooled, boiled water to stick it to the front of the body, with the straight side across the top of the bust. Cut to size using a craft knife. Repeat to make the back section of the bodice. Place the upper body into a polystyrene block to dry.

GROOM'S UPPER BODY

18 Repeat steps 8–15 to create the groom's head and upper body in the same way as for the bride. However, make the brow bone and jaw line more pronounced, leave the chest flat and paint the lips with a mixture of Rose and Chestnut paste food colours.

19 To make the hair, colour some white modelling paste with Marigold and Chestnut paste colours to create a blonde hair colour for the groom. Using the same technique as for the bride's hair, roll a ball of paste that is 1cm (³⁄₈") in diameter and stick it to the head. Texture the hair using the pointed end of a Dresden tool.

20 For the shirt, roll out some white modelling paste thinly so it is large enough to cover the chest. Mark a line down the middle of the shirt and cut a small 'V' shape in the top so it will fit around the neck. Attach

the shirt to the front of the groom's torso using a little cooled, boiled water.

21 Cut a 5mm (¼") wide strip for the collar, attach it around the neck and trim to size. Roll out a small amount of black modelling paste thinly and cut out two small triangles for the bow tie. Attach the triangles to the front of the collar using a little cooled, boiled water. Leave the body to dry in a polystyrene block.

22 Roll two small balls of skin-coloured paste and flatten them slightly between your finger and thumb. Use a craft knife to make a small cut in one side to bring out a thumb. Mark the fingers on the hand with the knife, making sure not to cut all the way through the paste otherwise the fingers will be too fragile. Smooth down and round off the tips of each finger. Add detail to the back of the hand with a Dresden tool, then leave the hands to dry. You only need to make the hands for the groom as you will make the sleeves later.

23 Roll a sausage of black modelling paste that is approximately 1cm (³⁄₈") in diameter and 4cm (1½") long. Taper each end of the sausage and cut in half for the shoes. Take one half of the sausage, flatten one side against the work surface to create the sole and shape the toe into a point. Use a craft knife to mark across the heel of the sole. Make a hole in the top of the shoe where you will attach it to the trousers. Repeat to make the second shoe.

CARVING THE CAKES

24 Use a serrated knife to cut the 30.5cm (12") square cake into three pieces as pictured. The two smaller pieces of cake will make the aeroplane's fuselage and the larger part will make the clouds that hide the stand.

25 Position the aeroplane armature so it sits diagonally across the cake drum, making sure that the wings don't come over the edge of the board.

26 Cut the largest piece of cake in half and place the pieces on either side of the stand, allowing approximately a 5mm (¼") gap between the cake and the armature. Trim away the corners of the cake and position them so they hide the front of the stand. Remove the armature so you have more space to carve the clouds into shape. Use a large, serrated knife to round off the edges of the cake so it resembles the fluffiness of a cloud. You don't need to be precise with the cloud shapes, as long as you hide the armature.

27 To build up height and ensure the stand is hidden, cut the 20.5cm (8") square cake in half and place the pieces on top of the first layer of carved cake. Continue carving the cloud shape in the same way as before. The cake should be roughly circular and should hide the stand completely.

28 Layer the remaining two smaller pieces of cake with buttercream to make the fuselage. Turn the cake on its side

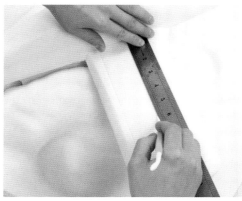

and use a large, serrated knife to carve out the shape of the aeroplane. At the wider end of the fuselage, cut a piece out of the front of the cake to make the nose and then round off the edges.

29 Place the cake on top of the armature and check that it fits on the stand. If you are happy with the shape, position the plane on the board and crumb-coat the whole cake with buttercream, including the clouds (see page 14).

COVERING THE CAKES

30 Remove the aeroplane cake and the stand. Roll out approximately 2kg (4lb 6½oz) of Bridal White sugarpaste to approximately 5mm (¼") thick, so you have a piece of paste that is large enough to cover both the clouds and the cake drum. Brush the exposed cake drum with cooled, boiled water, then cover the clouds and the board all in one go (see page 17).

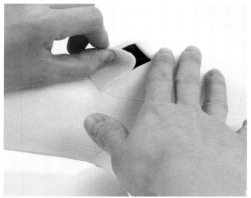

31 Spread a layer of royal icing over the inside of the cloud cake where the plane will sit, place the aeroplane cake on its armature then position it back on the drum in between the clouds. The royal icing will help to hold it in position so that it doesn't tip over when you're covering the cake.

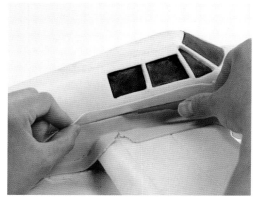
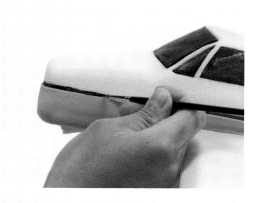

32 Roll out some Tuxedo Black sugarpaste to 2mm (¹⁄₁₆") thick and cut out a long strip to stick around the cockpit and back along both sides of the plane where the windows will be. Stick a rectangle of black paste over the nose where the propellers will be attached.

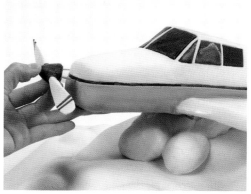

33 Roll out 1kg (2lb 3¼oz) of Bridal White sugarpaste to approximately 3mm (¹⁄₈") thick so that it is large enough to cover the fuselage and the wings. Dampen the top part of the wings with a little cooled, boiled water and cover the fuselage and the wings in one go (see page 17). Trim away any excess paste.

34 Mark the detail on the wings using a ruler and Dresden tool.

35 Use a Dresden tool to mark out all the windows, the cockpit and the nose where the propellers will sit. Cut along the marks with a craft knife and peel back the white paste to reveal the black paste underneath.

36 To make the blue stripe, roll out the Lullaby Blue sugarpaste very thinly into a strip that is as long as the aeroplane. Measure approximately 2cm (¾") up from the bottom of the plane and dampen a strip along the side of the plane. Stick the sugarpaste along the side and cut it straight using a ruler and a craft knife. Trim away any excess paste. Repeat on the other side of the plane.

37 Cover the tips of the wings and the tail wing with the remaining Lullaby Blue sugarpaste. Use a no. 2 paintbrush and Bulrush paste food colour to paint a 3mm (⅛") wide line above the blue strip on the fuselage and inside the blue wing tips.

38 Mark out the writing freehand on the side of the aeroplane with a Dresden tool, or make your own lettering template if you prefer. Paint over the lettering with Bulrush paste food colour and a fine paintbrush, or use an edible food colour pen if you are less confident.

39 Insert the propeller in the front of the plane and the tail wing at the back of the fuselage and secure in place with royal icing.

BRIDE'S LOWER BODY

40 As the bride will be sitting on the cake, the skirt needs to be placed directly onto the aeroplane and the upper body assembled on the skirt. To make the skirt, roll a thick sausage of white modelling paste that is approximately 7.5cm (3") long and 2.5cm (1") in diameter. Flatten one end of the sausage with a small rolling pin to flare the paste. Roll out the flattened side more thinly then frill the edge by rolling a cocktail stick along it. Dab a little cooled, boiled water where the bride will sit on top of the aeroplane, place the skirt on the aeroplane and arrange it naturally.

41 Stick the upper body onto the skirt with a little cooled, boiled water. Roll out a little white modelling paste very thinly, making the paste approximately the same size as the first skirt. Frill the end of the paste as before and wrap the layer over the original skirt so the hem sits slightly higher.

BRIDE'S ARMS

42 Using some skin-coloured modelling paste, roll out a thin sausage that is approximately 5mm (¼") in diameter and 10cm (4") long. Cut the sausage in half to make two arms that are equal in size. Keep one sausage of paste in a sealed food-grade plastic bag so that it doesn't dry out whilst you are working on the first arm.

43 Flatten one end of the sausage between your fingers to make the hand, then pinch out the elbow and wrist. Follow step 22 to shape the hand and bring out the fingers.

44 Stick the left arm to the shoulder using a little cooled, boiled water and pose it so that the hand is touching the dress. The right arm will rest on the groom's body, so make and attach it after the groom is in place.

GROOM'S LOWER BODY

45 For the trousers, roll out a sausage of black modelling paste that is 1cm thick x 10cm long (³/₈" x 4"). Taper the sausage at both ends then fold it in half to make two legs. Use a ball tool to create sockets at the end of each leg for the shoes.

46 Dab a little cooled, boiled water where the groom is going to sit on the aeroplane. Position the trousers on the plane and use a Dresden tool to add folds and creases for a more natural look. Stick the shoes to the sockets using a little royal icing.

47 Secure the upper body onto the trousers using a little cooled, boiled water. Roll out some black modelling paste very thinly to approximately 6cm x 10cm (2³/₈" x 4") in size. Cut out the pieces of the jacket following the template. Stick the jacket pieces around the groom's torso using a little cooled, boiled water.

48 Roll a sausage of black modelling paste that is approximately 9cm long x 1cm thick (3½" x ³/₈"). Cut it in half, then taper the end of each arm and bend slightly at the elbow. Use a Dresden tool to add creases at the bend, then use a bone tool to make sockets for the hands. Dampen the sockets with a little cooled, boiled water and stick the hands inside. Stick the arms to the body also using a little cooled, boiled water.

FINISHING TOUCHES

49 Using the sausage of paste from step 42, model the bride's right arm in the same way as the left arm. Position the arm so that her right hand is resting on the groom's waist then stick it to the body with cooled, boiled water.

50 Model some small cloud shapes from Bridal White sugarpaste and attach them around the base to cover any exposed armature.

51 Mix five parts Edelweiss liquid food colour to one part Bluebell liquid food colour in an airbrush and spray lightly over the clouds, being careful to avoid the aeroplane.

52 Trim the cake drum with ivory ribbon to finish.

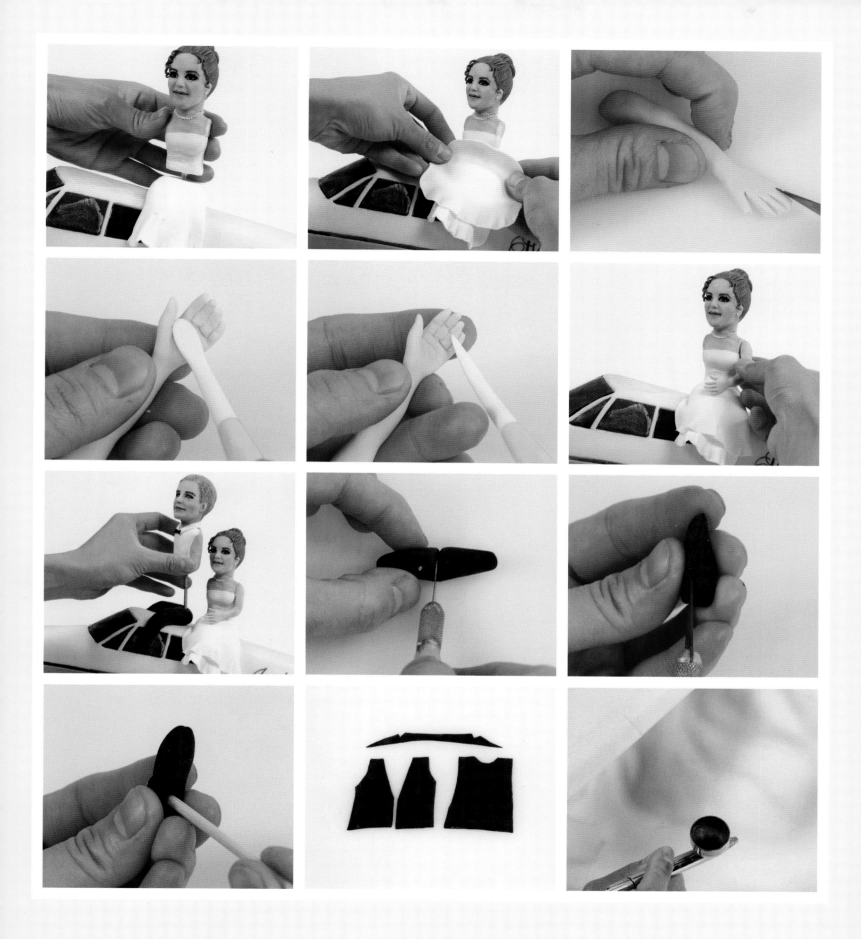

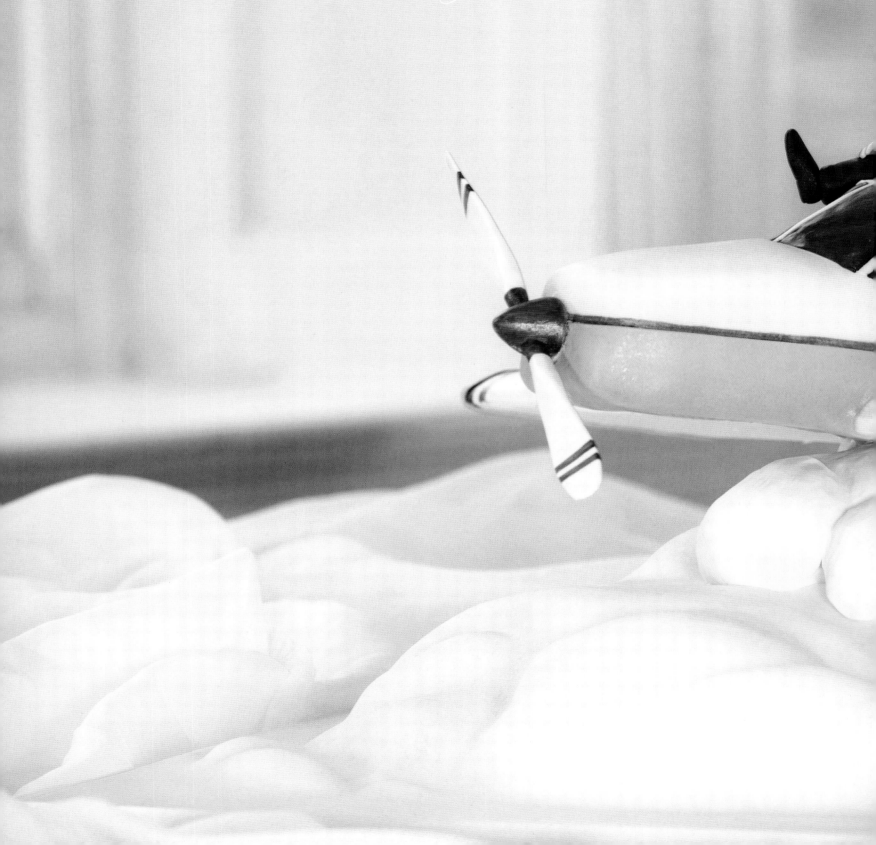

On the Wings of Love

SOMETHING OLD, SOMETHING NEW

I took inspiration from the popular saying, "Something old, something new, something borrowed, something blue, and a silver sixpence in her shoe" for this simple yet elegant bridal shower cake.

Size: approx. 30.5cm x 20.5cm x 10cm (12" x 8" x 4") | Serves 50

EDIBLES

30.5cm (12") square sponge cake

1 quantity of buttercream (see page 12)

SK Sugarpaste (rolled fondant): 2kg (4lb 6½oz) Bridal White

SK Sugar Florist Paste (SFP): 50g (1¾oz) White coloured with a touch of Bluegrass paste food colour, 5g (just under ¼oz) White coloured with a touch of Bulrush paste food colour, 50g (1¾oz) White coloured with a touch of Chestnut paste food colour

Modelling paste (sugarpaste + CMC, see page 12): 250g (8¾oz) Bridal White

SK Professional Paste Food Colours: Bluegrass, Bulrush (dark brown), Chestnut (soft beige)

SK Designer Bridal Satin Lustre Dust Food Colour: White Satin

SK Designer Metallic Lustre Dust Food Colours: Antique Gold, Light Silver

SK Confectioners' Glaze

EQUIPMENT

Basic equipment (see pages 6–9)

40.5cm (16") square cake drum (board)

Plastic cake dowel

Polystyrene block

Cattleya orchid petal cutter, from set of 3: 2cm (¾") (PME)

Round cutters: 1.8cm, 2cm, 2.2cm, 2.4cm (11/16", ¾", 7/8", 15/16")

Piping nozzles: nos. 0, 1

Wax paper or baking parchment

Piece of food-grade cardboard, e.g. a spare lid from a cake box

Satin ribbon: 1.68m (66") x 15mm (5/8") width champagne

Paintbrushes: nos. 0 (fine), 10 (flat) (SK)

Templates (see page 129)

CAKE

1 Cut the whole cake into four layers (see page 14). Cut the cake into two rectangles measuring 30.5cm x 20.5cm (12" x 8") and 10cm x 30.5cm (4" x 12"). Stack the 10cm (4") wide layers of cake side-by-side on top of the larger cake to make the height up to 10cm (4") overall. Fill each layer of cake, crumb-coat with buttercream and arrange on the cake drum.

2 Roll out some Bridal White sugarpaste to 5mm (¼") and cover the cake in sections following the technique on page 18. To create the shoe box lid, cover the top of the cake with a thin layer of white sugarpaste and use a smoother to create sharp edges. Use a clean ruler to mark the outline of the lid around each side of the cake and trim away any excess paste with a craft knife.

3 Roll out a thin layer of Bridal White sugarpaste and cover the cake drum in sections, to create a fabric effect (see page 16).

4 To decorate the corners of the lid, fit a piping bag with a no. 1 nozzle and fill ²/₃ full with royal icing. Pipe the same freehand design on two opposite corners of the top of the cake. Once the icing is dry, dilute some White Satin lustre dust with a little cooled, boiled water in a palette or small bowl and paint the whole lid with the mixture.

HIGH-HEELED SHOE

5 Trace around each of the shoe templates onto greaseproof or wax paper and cut them out with a pair of scissors. Copy the sole template again onto a piece of food-grade cardboard, such as a spare lid from a cake box or cereal box, and cut out with a craft knife. This template needs to be made of cardboard as it will be used as a temporary support whilst the sole is drying.

HEEL

6 Cut a plastic cake dowel to approximately 10cm (4") in length. Roll

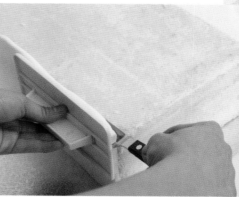
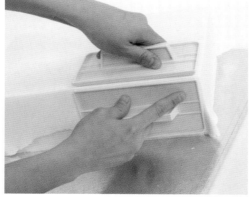
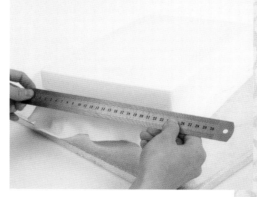

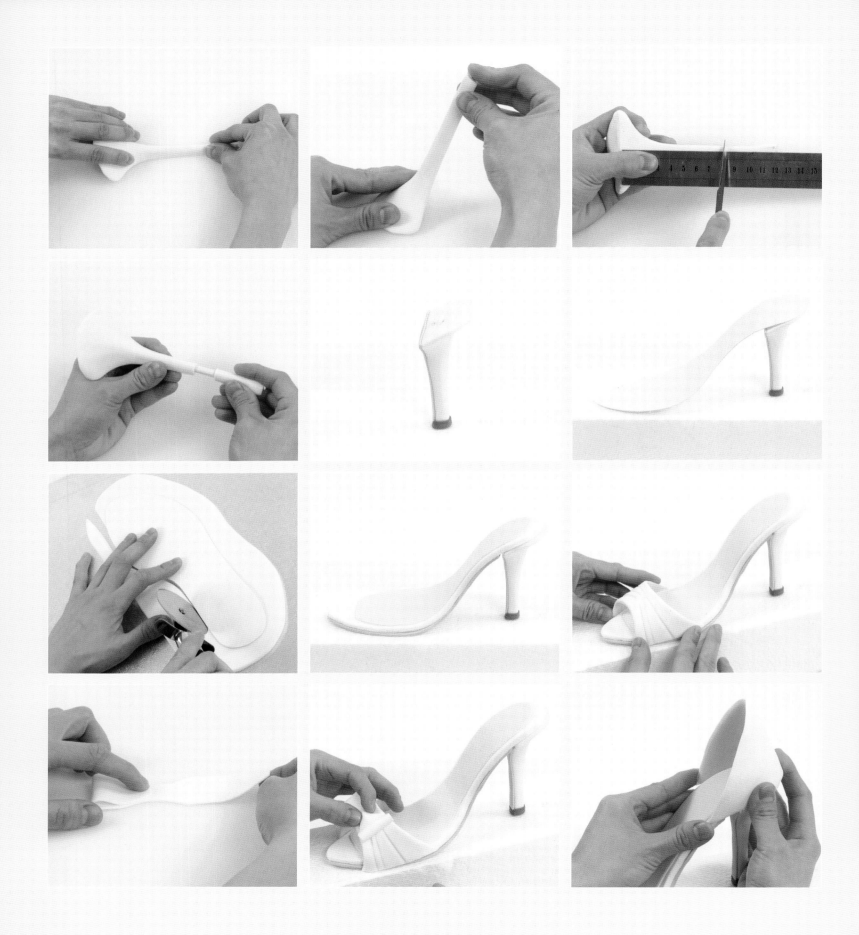

some white modelling paste into a ball that is approximately 5cm (2") in diameter, then model into a pointed cone shape. Bring out the point of the cone further to make the stiletto heel, which should be approximately 8cm (3¹/₈") long. Insert the dowel into the longer piece of paste, then continue to lengthen the paste until you cover the dowel completely.

7 Rest the top of the heel on a flat surface, tilt the heel slightly, then adjust the dowelled part of the heel to the natural angle for a high-heeled shoe. Cut approximately 1.5cm (⁵/₈") of sugarpaste from the narrow end of the heel to expose the dowel.

8 Roll out some light Chestnut-coloured SFP to 2mm (¹/₁₆") thick, then attach the paste to the inside (the flat side) of the heel with a little cooled, boiled water. Use a cutting wheel to trim the paste to fit the shape of the heel.

9 Roll a small ball of the Chestnut-coloured SFP, flatten the ball between your fingers and push the paste onto the dowel so it sits at the base of the heel.

10 To check the heel is at the correct angle, turn it the right way up and insert the exposed dowel into a block of polystyrene. Rest the cardboard sole armature on top of the heel, then bend the armature into the right shape for the shoe and adjust the heel until you achieve the correct angle. Place the heel on its side on a flat surface and leave to dry.

SOLE

11 Roll out some White SFP to approximately 3mm (¹/₈") thick, place the paper sole template on the paste and cut around it with a cutting wheel (or pizza wheel) to make the middle part of the sole.

12 For the outer sole, roll out some light Chestnut-coloured SFP to

approximately 2mm (¹/₁₆") thick, place the outer sole template on the paste and cut it out. Stick it to the bottom of the middle part of the sole with a little cooled, boiled water.

13 Roll out some more light Chestnut-coloured SFP very thinly and cut around the insole template. Stick the insole on top of the white sole and then run a stitching tool around the very edge of the insole.

14 Once the heel has dried, stand it up on the polystyrene block and rest the cardboard sole armature on the upright heel as before. Place the sole onto the cardboard and leave to dry completely. When the sole is dry, remove the cardboard armature and stick the top end of the sole to the heel with a little royal icing. Leave it to set in place.

TOE STRAP

15 Roll out some White SFP and some light Chestnut-coloured SFP, ensuring that the coloured SFP is rolled out as thin as possible so it won't show through once they are rolled together. Put one piece of paste on top of the other and roll out together to make double-sided paste (see page 18). Place the toe strap template on the paste, cut around it and then add the fold details across the strap using a pizza wheel. Use a little cooled, boiled water to attach the ends of the strap to the sole at the front of the shoe. Scrunch up some kitchen paper and place it under the arch to support it, then leave to dry completely.

16 To make the bow, roll out some White SFP to approximately 2mm (¹/₁₆") thick. Use a cutting wheel and a ruler to cut a strip of paste that is approximately 2.5cm (1") wide and approximately 7.5cm (3") long. For the knot, make another strip of paste that is approximately half the width of the first strip. Dampen the middle of the long ribbon with a little cooled, boiled water, fold both ends into the middle and stick in place. Repeat the process to make a second, smaller bow, then place the second bow on top of the first and attach the smaller strip of paste over the join.

Once the toe strap is dry, stick the bow to the strap with a little cooled, boiled water.

COUNTER (HEEL SUPPORT)

17 Make up some more double-sided paste with White and Chestnut-coloured SFP (see step 15). Place the counter template on the paste and cut around it with a pizza wheel. Bend the paste into shape and use cooled, boiled water to stick the bottom of the paste to the very back of the sole. Support the paste with scrunched-up kitchen paper if necessary.

FINISHING THE SHOE

18 Mix some White Satin lustre dust with a little confectioners' glaze and paint over the whole shoe, except for the outer sole and the insole. Leave to dry completely.

19 Once dry, remove the shoe from the block of polystyrene then carefully cut off the extra piece of dowel with a pair of wire cutters.

GARTER

20 Roll out some Bluegrass-coloured SFP very thinly, then cut out two strips measuring approximately 25cm x 3cm (10" x 1⅛") in size. Use a cocktail stick to frill one edge of each strip then use your fingers to fold the paste into larger frills. Make sure that the final length of each strip is approximately 11.5cm (4½").

21 Roll out some more Bluegrass-coloured SFP to approximately 3mm (⅛") thick and cut out another strip that is 11.5cm x 2cm (4½" x ¾") in size. Use a Dresden tool to mark tight folds all the way along the paste. Cut the length to 11.5cm (4½") again with a craft knife, as the paste will have stretched as you have been working with it. To assemble the garter, fold each of the frilled strips in half, then place the thicker strip between the frilled strips and stick in place with a little cooled, boiled water. Leave to dry.

22 To decorate the garter, thinly roll out a small piece of White SFP and cut out a long, 3mm (⅛") wide strip. Fold it into a bow and place in the centre of the garter. Roll seven small balls of White SFP, arrange them to look like a brooch in the centre of the bow and stick them in place with a little royal icing.

23 Once the garter is dry, mix some White Satin lustre dust with a little confectioners' glaze in a palette or small bowl and use a fine paintbrush to paint over the whole garter, including the pearl decoration.

CORSAGE

24 Roll out a piece of White SFP very thinly and cut out 16 petals from the paste with the 2cm (¾") orchid petal cutter. Pinch one end of each petal together, then leave them to dry on a piece of kitchen paper. Make seven 5mm (¼") balls from some more White SFP then leave them to dry.

25 Take a small amount of White SFP and roll it into a ball that is 2.5cm (1") in diameter. Flatten one side of the ball and place this side down on the work surface. Position nine petals so that they are equally spaced around the circle of paste and attach with a little cooled, boiled water. Attach seven more petals on top of the first layer in the same way, so each petal sits between the petals underneath. Leave all the petals to set in place.

26 Make seven balls of White SFP that are 5mm (¼") in diameter and attach them to the centre of the corsage with a little royal icing. Leave to dry completely then paint the pearls with the diluted White Satin dust mixture.

27 Fit a small piping bag with a no. 0 nozzle, fill ⅔ full with white royal icing and pipe a random filigree pattern over each petal. Allow the royal icing to dry, then mix some Light Silver lustre dust with a little confectioners' glaze and paint every petal with the mixture.

RINGS

28 To make the first wedding ring, roll out some White SFP and cut out a circle from the paste with a 1.8cm (¹¹/₁₆") round cutter, then cut another circle outside the first with a 2.2cm (⅞") round cutter. Cut out the second ring as before, but use the 2cm (¾") and 2.4cm (¹⁵/₁₆") round cutters instead. Once the rings are dry, mix some Antique Gold lustre dust with a little confectioners' glaze and paint each ring.

ASSEMBLY

29 Position the shoe, corsage and rings on top of the cake and secure in place with royal icing. Attach the garter to the front of the board with a dab of royal icing. To finish, trim the edge of the board with ivory ribbon.

Something Old, Something New

ST. BRIDE'S CHURCH

This grand cake design is inspired by St. Bride's, the world-famous church in the City of London which is recognisable for its wedding cake-style tower. With its magnificent architecture designed by Sir Christopher Wren and its elegant grandeur, this showstopping centrepiece would be perfect for an opulent wedding ceremony.

Size approx. 40.5cm x 20.5cm x 76cm (16" x 8" x 30") | Serves 125

EDIBLES

4 x 20.5cm (8") square sponge cakes, layered and filled (see page 14)

4 quantities of buttercream (see page 12)

SK Sugarpaste (rolled fondant): 3.5kg (7½lb) Vintage Ivory

Modelling paste (sugarpaste + CMC, see page 12): 800g (1lb 12oz) Vintage Ivory

SK Sugar Florist Paste (SFP): 100g (3½oz) Cream

350g (12¼oz) SK Instant Mix Royal Icing

SK Professional Paste Food Colours: Bulrush (dark brown), Edelweiss (white)

SK Professional Liquid Food Colours (for airbrushing): Chestnut (soft beige), Marigold (tangerine)

SK Quality Food Colour (QFC) Liquid: Black

SK Edible Metallic Paint: Gold

EQUIPMENT

Basic equipment (see page 6–9)

Rectangular cake drums (boards): 35.5cm x 61cm (14" x 24") and 30.5cm x 51cm (12" x 20")

51cm x 76cm (20" x 30") pieces of 1cm and 5mm (³/₈" and ¼") thick foamboard

48cm (19") x 1.8cm (¹¹/₁₆") diameter wooden dowel

Electric drill with 2mm (¹/₁₆") drill bit

5cm (2") long screw

4 x 'hidden' pillars (Wilton)

8 plastic dowels

19cm long x 4cm diameter (7½" x 1½") PVC pipe, covered with food sealing wrap

Round cutters: 4.2cm, 5.8cm (1¹¹/₁₆", 2⁵/₁₆")

Round medium cutters, set of 3: 1.7cm, 2.2cm, 2.6cm (¹¹/₁₆", ⁷/₈", 1¹/₁₆") (Kitbox)

Round plunger cutter set: 1cm, 1.2cm, 1.5cm (³/₈", ⁷/₁₆", ⁵/₈") (PME)

Miniature brickwork embosser (PC)

Round paintbrushes: nos. 0, 3 (SK)

Satin ribbon: 2m (79") x 15mm (⁵/₈") width black

Templates and diagrams (see pages 130–131)

ST. BRIDE'S CHURCH

ARMATURES

1 Enlarge the spire (A), tower (B) and back façade (D) templates by 200% using a photocopier (see pages 130–131).

2 Glue the smaller rectangular cake drum centrally on top of the larger one with craft glue and leave to dry.

3 Using diagram 1 on page 130, mark the point where you will attach the long wooden dowel on the drum. Drill a screw up through the bottom of the base drum at the marked point. Use a 2mm (1/16") drill bit to drill into one end of the wooden dowel. Cover the wooden dowel with cake board foil and screw it in place at the mark.

4 Draw out the shape of the bottom and top tier boards onto 1cm (3/8") foamboard, following the dimensions specified in diagram 2. Cut out the shapes with a Stanley knife then mark where the long dowel will go through each board. Cover them completely in food sealing wrap and make a hole in each piece of foamboard with a wooden stake.

5 For the tower, cut out three 10cm (4") squares from the 5mm (1/4") foamboard and make a hole in the centre of each square. Cover all of the boards completely with food sealing wrap.

SPIRE

6 Cut out two 7cm (2¾") diameter circles from the 1cm (3/8") thick foamboard. Draw around the end of the PVC pipe onto one of the circles and cut out the inner circle with a craft knife. Make a hole in the other circle using a wooden stake then glue the two together with craft glue. Cover the base of the circle with a thin layer of white modelling paste, leaving the bigger hole exposed on top.

7 Cover the PVC pipe with food sealing wrap then with a thin layer of ivory modelling paste, leaving 1cm (3/8") exposed

at one end. Insert the exposed pipe into the circular base and secure with royal icing: this will be the main core for the spire. Leave it to dry.

8 Roll out some of the ivory modelling paste very thinly and cut out a strip that is 4cm x 20.5cm (1½" x 8") in size using a cutting wheel. Use a ruler and a craft knife to cut the strip into eight 4cm x 2.5cm (1½" x 1") panels. Cut out a hole approximately 5mm (¼") from the top of each panel using a 1.5cm (5/8") round plunger cutter. Cut a straight line from each side of the circle down to the bottom of the paste and discard the excess to make an arch opening. Repeat the same process for the seven remaining panels. Leave them to dry flat on a spare board.

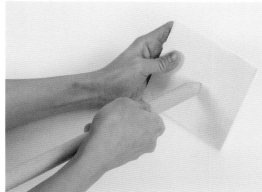

9 Repeat step 8 to make a second set of eight panels for the middle tier that are 2.3cm x 4.5cm (15/16" x 1¾") in size, using a 1.2cm (7/16") round plunger cutter. Make another set of eight panels that are 1.8cm x 3cm (11/16" x 1⅛") in size, using a 1cm (3/8") round plunger cutter.

10 Roll out some ivory modelling paste to approximately 5mm (¼") thick, then use the octagon templates and a paring knife to cut out two different-sized octagons. Cut out a circle from the centre of each using a 4.2cm (1 11/16") round cutter, then cut them in half so they will fit around the spire core later.

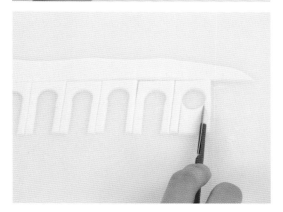

11 For the top of the spire, roll a 2.5cm (1") thick sausage of ivory modelling paste. Cut it to approximately 2cm (¾") long and trim down the sides with a craft knife to get an octagonal cylinder shape.

12 Cut another piece from the same sausage of paste that is approximately 5cm (2") long. Roll one end more thinly to make a cone shape for the tip. Make a very small ball and a tiny pointed sausage to sit on the top of the spire. Use the spire template as a guide for the measurements.

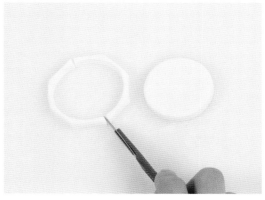

13 Leave all the pieces on a spare cake board to dry completely.

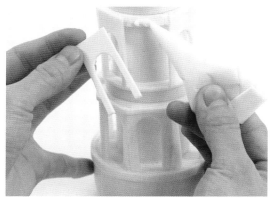

TOP TIP

Always use royal icing to stick dried pieces of sugar work together and pre-boiled water or edible glue to secure softer pieces in place.

14 Following the spire template as a guide, stick all the dry pieces together with royal icing.

15 Add the final details to the spire by rolling out some more modelling paste to approximately 2mm (1/16") thick and adding strips around the top of each section, using the spire template as a guide. Stick them in place and cut to size with a craft knife.

WINDOWS

16 Roll out some Cream SFP very thinly, place the side arch window template (C1) on the paste and use a cutting wheel to cut out the shape. Use a paintbrush to dampen the edges of the window with a little pre-boiled water, then cut out another window of the same shape and stick it on top of the first. Use a craft knife to cut 2mm (1/16") inside the edge of the window, taking care not to cut through both pieces of paste. Peel away the inner piece of paste to create a window frame, leaving the first piece of paste behind for the window pane. Make six of these then leave to dry completely on a spare board.

17 Follow step 16 to make all the remaining windows from the templates: you will need three back windows (C2) and four tower windows (C3).

18 For the larger circular windows, roll out some Cream SFP very thinly and cut out 13 circles using a 2.6cm (1 1/16") round cutter. Cut out the inside of each circle with a 2.2cm (7/8") round cutter to make 13 frames. Make two smaller circular frames in the same way using the 2.2cm (7/8") and 1.7cm (11/16")

round cutters. Leave the frames to dry.

19 To make two rectangular windows for the front of the base tier, roll out some Cream SFP very thinly and cut out four rectangles that are 2cm (3/4") x 3.5cm (1 3/8") in size. Following step 16, stick one rectangle on top of another, cut 2mm (1/16") inside the edge to make the frame and peel away the paste. Leave them to dry.

20 For the rectangular window at the front of the tower, use template B to measure out the window then cut it out of Cream SFP. Continue to make the window in the same way as for the rectangular windows in step 19.

21 Use a no. 3 round paintbrush with Bulrush paste food colour to paint all the window panes, being careful to leave the frames unpainted. Use a no. 0 paintbrush to paint fine lines over the panes with Edelweiss paste food colour.

DOOR

22 Roll out some ivory modelling paste to approximately 3mm (1/8") thick and cut out a 4cm x 6cm (1 1/2" x 2 3/8") panel. Cut the top using a 5.8cm (2 5/16") round cutter to make an arch and mark a line across the base of the arch with a craft knife.

23 Mark out a rectangle on the paste that is approximately 2cm x 3cm (3/4" x 1 1/8") in size in the middle of the panel. Draw a line down the centre of the rectangle to make two doors and mark a 3mm (1/8") frame around them. Roll out a thin strip of ivory modelling paste that is 8mm wide x 7cm long (3/8" x 2 3/4"), attach it over the curve of the door and leave to dry.

WALL BUTTRESSES

24 Roll out some ivory modelling paste to approximately 5mm (1/4") thick. Place the buttress template on the paste

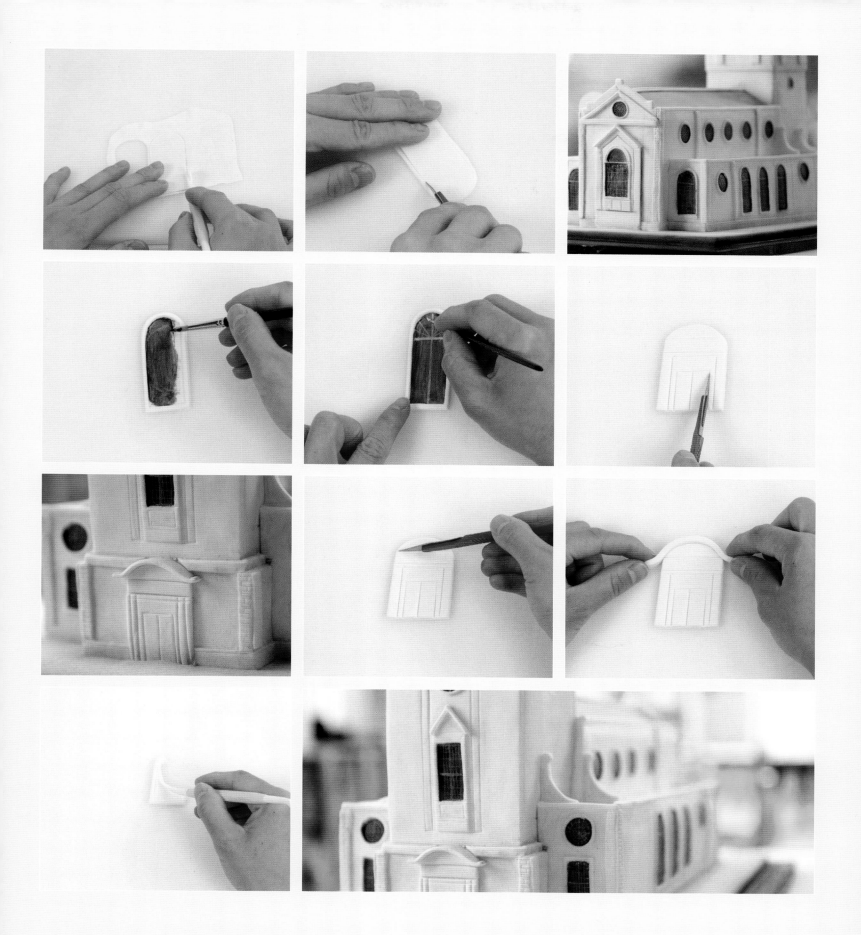

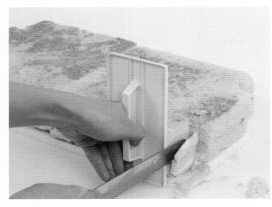

and use a blunt knife to cut around it. Use a Dresden tool to add the triangular detail to the centre of the buttress. Repeat to make two pairs of wall buttresses. Allow them to dry.

CAKES

25 Place two 20.5cm (8") square cakes side by side on the base building board and stick the sides together with buttercream. Level the tops of the cakes with a large, serrated knife and trim the sides following the shape of the board. Use a cake smoother to help you cut the straight edges. Crumb-coat the whole tier with buttercream (see page 14).

26 Cut the third 20.5cm (8") square cake in half to make two 10cm x 20.5cm (4" x 8") cakes. Stick the ends together with buttercream to make a long strip of cake and crumb-coat.

27 For the roof line, mark approximately 6.5cm (2½") up from the base of the longer sides of the cake. Mark the halfway line along the length of the top of the cake. To make the angled roof shape, use a serrated knife to cut away the cake between the line at the top and the line at the side. Do not cut all the way along the cake: leave 10cm (4") flat at one end for the tower to sit on. Crumb-coat the whole tier with buttercream (see page 14).

28 Cut the remaining 20.5cm (8") cake into four equal squares and place the pieces of cake on each of the square tower foamboards from step 5. Stack each cake and board on top of each other so that the overall height of the tower is 20.5cm (8").

29 To put the base tier on the armature, lift the cake onto its board and make a hole at the mark with a 'hidden' pillar. Position the hole over the dowel and push the cake on its board gently down the dowel and secure it to the board with royal icing. Insert eight dowels into the bottom tier (see page 18), then sit the roof on top and secure in place with royal icing. Place a 'hidden' pillar down the dowel so it sits inside the cake and supports

the tower, then gently push the first tier of the tower down onto the pillar. Repeat with the remaining three layers for the tower, supporting each tier with a 'hidden' pillar.

30 Roll out some Vintage Ivory sugarpaste to approximately 5mm (¼") thick and cover the cake, roof, tower and drums one section at a time, rather than covering it all in one go (see page 18).

DECORATING THE BUILDING

31 Roll out some ivory modelling paste to approximately 3mm (⅛") thick. Place the back façade template (D) on the paste and cut around the outline using a cutting wheel. Using the template as a guide, mark on all the line detail with a Dresden tool and a ruler. Stick the façade to the back of the building using a little cooled, boiled water.

32 Cut along the dotted lines on template D to make a template for the back window. Roll out some ivory modelling paste to approximately 2mm (¹⁄₁₆") thick, place the window template on the paste and cut around it with a cutting wheel. Mark on the line detail using a Dresden tool and a ruler, then secure it in place on the back façade. Use Bulrush and Edelweiss paste food colours to paint the window pane.

33 Roll out some ivory modelling paste to approximately 2mm (¹⁄₁₆") thick and use the back façade template to cut the paste to size for the cornicing (eaves).

34 Roll out some more ivory modelling paste to the same thickness and use the tower template to cut the paste to size for the cornice decoration. Repeat the decoration around all four sides of the tower.

35 Using the tower template as a guide, attach the tower windows then use a clean ruler to mark straight lines across each side of the tower.

36 For the plinth, roll out some Vintage Ivory sugarpaste very thinly and cut a long strip that is approximately 1cm (3/8") wide. Stick it along the base of the side of the building with a little cooled, boiled water and trim to size. Repeat to create a plinth that runs all the way around the base of the building.

37 Repeat the step above to make the parapet wall that runs around the top of the bottom tier of the building. Make the ridge that runs along the top of the roof in the same way using a 5mm (1/4") wide strip.

38 Roll out some ivory sugarpaste very thinly and emboss it with a brick pattern using the embosser. Cut out some 1cm (3/8") wide strips from the embossed paste, stick them down all the corners of the building and trim to size.

39 Attach four larger circular windows along each of the long sides of the top tier. Stick two embossed strips down either side of the top tier building and one down the side of the base tier building, following the picture as a guide.

40 Stick the two smaller circular frames on opposite sides of the tower. Use Bulrush and Edelweiss paste food colours to paint the window panes directly onto the cake.

41 Use template B as a guide to position the rectangular window at the front of the tower and attach with a little cooled, boiled water.

42 Stick two smaller rectangular windows either side of the entrance at the front of the bottom tier, so they sit approximately 2cm (3/4") up from the base. Attach the round windows approximately 1cm (3/8") above the rectangular windows.

43 Attach three arch windows along each side of the base tier: align the middle window with the central circular window on the top tier and stick the other arch windows 2cm (3/4") either side. Stick a round window beside the arches towards the back of the building.

44 Attach the three arched windows to the back of the building. Cut approximately 5mm (1/4") wide strips to articulate the building using template D as a guide.

45 Secure two wall buttresses either side of the top of the base tier using a little royal icing.

AIRBRUSHING

46 Airbrush the roof using Chestnut liquid colour, being careful not to spray the ridge.

47 Mix five parts Chestnut to one part Black liquid food colour to achieve a dark brown. Carefully airbrush the inside of the spire (the core) with the dark brown colour. Spray the larger cake drum with the same colour.

48 Lightly airbrush all the walls with Marigold liquid food colour.

ATTACHING THE SPIRE

49 Place the spire down over the dowel and secure in place with royal icing. Paint the ball and spike at the top of the spire with edible Gold paint.

50 Trim the edge of the larger cake drum with black ribbon.

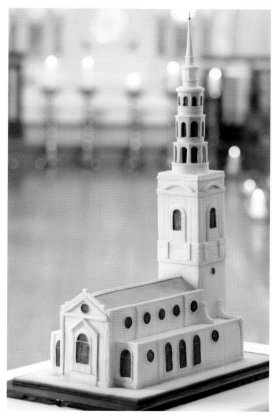

TOP TIP

The total height of the cake including the spire will be approximately 76cm (30") tall so, if you don't have enough space in the car to transport the cake, the spire can be attached once the cake is in situ. You will need to transport the cake and the spire in separate boxes.

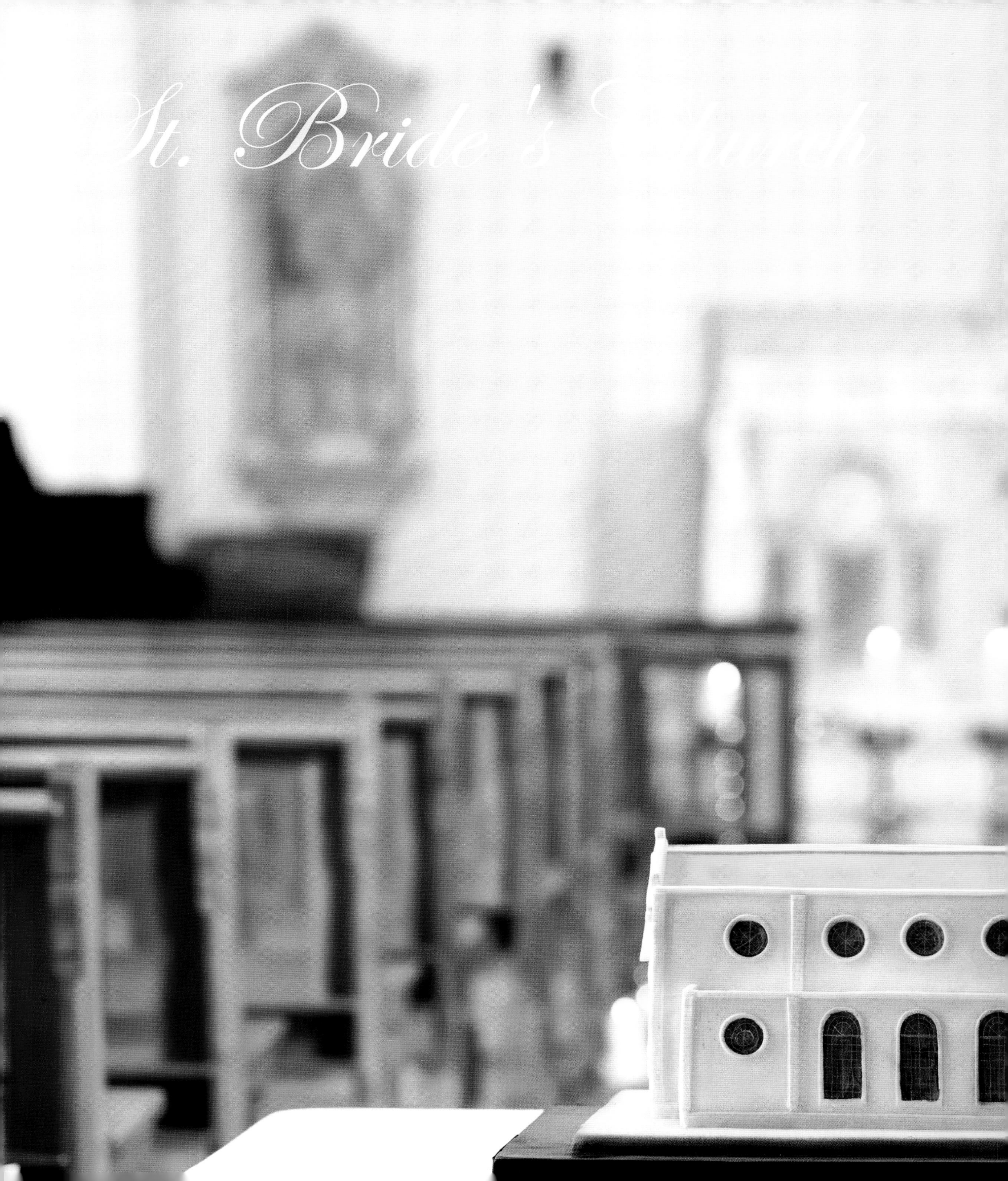
St. Bride's Church

FIRST LOVE

I remember when I was little I had a teddy which I adored – I loved dressing her as a bride and my friend dressed her teddy as the groom. Evoking nostalgic memories of childhood, this teddy bear cake design is a charming and romantic way to represent the newlyweds.

Size approx. 51cm x 51cm x 40.5cm (20" x 20" x 16") | Serves 100

EDIBLES

Square sponge cakes: 2 x 30.5cm (12"), 2 x 15cm (6")

4 quantities of buttercream (see page 12)

½ quantity of crisped rice cereal mix (see page 12)

SK Sugarpaste (rolled fondant): 2.5kg (5lb 8¼oz) Bridal White, 2.5kg (5lb 8¼oz) Mocha Cream

Modelling paste (sugarpaste + CMC, see page 12): 250g (8¾oz) Tuxedo Black

SK Sugar Florist Paste (SFP, gum paste): 100g (3½oz) White

350g (12¼oz) SK Instant Mix Royal Icing

SK Professional Paste Food Colours: Bulrush (dark brown), Chestnut (soft beige)

SK Designer Bridal Satin Lustre Dust Food Colours: Double Cream, White Satin

SK Professional Liquid Food Colours (for airbrushing): Bulrush (dark brown), Marigold (tangerine), Teddy Bear Brown

SK Confectioners' Glaze

SK Cellulose Gum (CMC)

EQUIPMENT

Basic equipment (see pages 6–9)

2 x 51cm (20") square cake drums (boards)

2 x 33cm long x 1.8cm diameter (13" x ¾") wooden dowels

51cm x 76cm (20" x 30") piece of 5mm (¼") thick foamboard

Electric drill with 2mm ($^{1}/_{16}$") drill bit

2 x 5cm (2") long screws

7 x 20.5cm (8") long plastic cake dowels

6 x 'hidden' pillars (Wilton)

Paintbrushes: nos. 2, 10 (flat) (SK)

Floral drape-effect textured rolling pin (JEM)

Piping nozzle: no. 3

Satin ribbon: 2.05m (81") x 25mm (1") width ivory

Templates and diagrams (see pages 132–133)

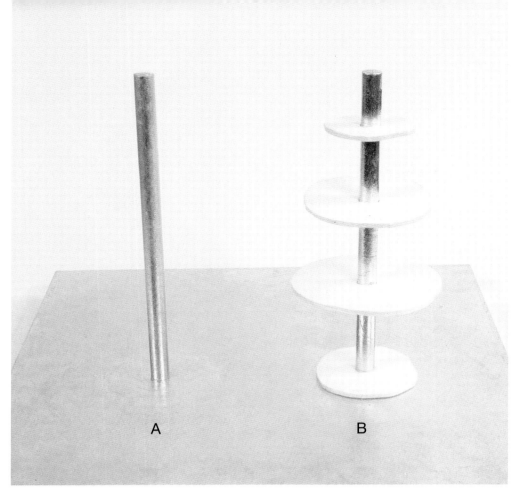

A

B

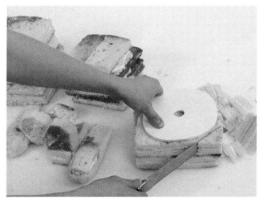

ARMATURES

1   Glue the two square cake drums on top of each other with craft glue and mark the dowel points on the back of the board, following the board diagram on page 132. Insert a screw at each dowel point from underneath the board, so the pointed end will stick out of the top. Use a 2mm (1/16") drill bit to drill into one end of each wooden dowel and wrap them both in cake board foil. Fix the dowels into the screws on the cake boards until they are secured in place, see above (A).

2   Draw the four armature templates onto the 5mm (¼") foamboard and cut them out with a craft knife. Repeat to make two sets of foamboard armatures, one set for each teddy bear. Make a hole in the middle of each armature with a wooden stake. Wrap all the separate pieces in food sealing wrap so they are completely covered. Check that the foamboard circles fit on the central column as shown above (B) then remove the circles.

CARVING THE CAKE

3   Layer and fill both 30.5cm (12") square cakes with buttercream and divide each cake into four 15cm (6") squares.

4   To carve the cake, place the middle tier armature under a 15cm (6") square of cake and place the top tier armature on top as a guide. Use a serrated knife to carve the cake into a curved shape between the two boards. Repeat for the bottom layer with the bottom tier armature under another 15cm (6") square cake and the middle tier armature on top. For the top tier, place the armature under a third square of cake and the head armature on top. For each teddy, you will have three layers of cake for the body and one layer for the head.

5   Cut one of the 15cm (6") square cakes into four sections, following the diagram to make a section for the legs, arms and an additional layer for the head (see page 130). Round off the edges of the legs and arms and

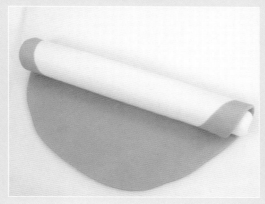

crumb-coat each piece (see page 14). Save the trimmings for the next step.

6 Stack the leftover pieces from the 15cm (6") cakes on the remaining squares of cake from step 3 to add extra volume to the top of the heads. Round off the edges and make the heads roughly spherical. Leave a section of cake sticking out at the front of the head and shape it into a small snout, then crumb-coat each head.

7 Place the bottom layer of the body on the corresponding foamboard, make a hole in the centre of the cake with a 'hidden' pillar and push it down onto one of the dowels on the cake drum. Insert three plastic dowels into the bottom layer to support the layers above (see page 18). Repeat for the middle and top tiers, but do not dowel the top layer of cake. Place the legs next to the body to check they are in proportion, trimming them down if necessary.

Once you are happy with the size, crumb-coat the body and legs all together. Repeat for the second teddy bear.

8 Arrange the arms and the head together with the body and legs to check the proportions, then crumb-coat them as well. Carefully remove all the cake parts from the main board and place them on spare cake boards. Leave them in the fridge or freezer if possible until they are ready to be covered.

COVERING THE CAKES

9 Roll out 500g (1lb 1¾oz) of Mocha Cream sugarpaste and 500g (1lb 1¾oz) of Bridal White sugarpaste then use the double-sided coating technique on page 18 to cover the body. Place the paste over the top of the body and smooth down with cake smoothers, making sure the paste fits

to the curved shape of the cake. Uncover the hole at the top of the body. Trim any excess sugarpaste from around the bottom and place the body down onto one of the dowels. Secure the cake to the board with a little royal icing then repeat for the second teddy bear.

10 While the sugarpaste is still soft, texture both of the bodies with a Dresden tool to create a fur effect. For the groom teddy, hold the Dresden tool vertically and move the pointed end gently down the paste to make strokes that are approximately 1cm (³/₈") long. For the bride teddy, make the strokes slightly longer to approximately 2cm (¾"), in order to give her a softer, more feminine appearance. Whilst you are texturing the body, vary the angle of each stroke slightly so that the texture looks more natural.

11 Cover each of the legs with Mocha Cream sugarpaste. Mark a seam

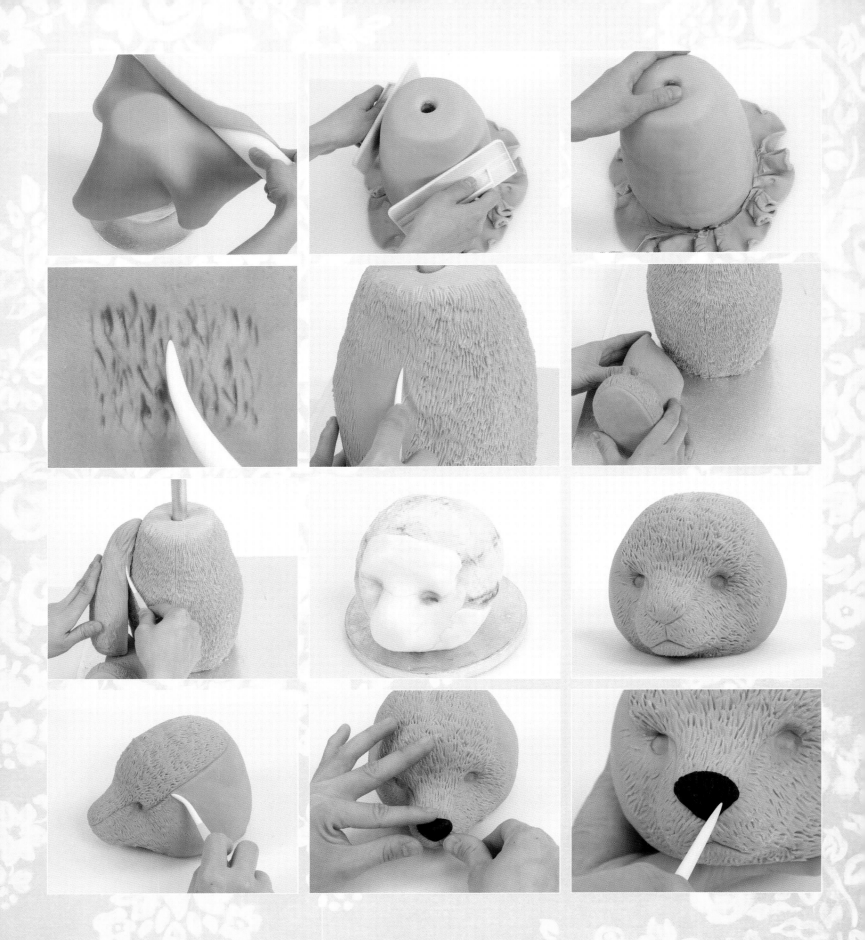

line around the bottom of the feet with a Dresden tool and texture the leg in the same way as for the body. Draw shorter strokes down the bottom of the feet using medium pressure to create a different texture. Stick the legs to the base of the body using a little cooled, boiled water.

12 Working on one arm at a time, cover them each with 150g (5¼oz) of Mocha Cream sugarpaste, ensuring not to leave any cake exposed. Dampen the back of the arm with a little pre-boiled water then stick the arm vertically down the side of the body. Texture the arms as for the body and draw seam lines around the end to mark out the hands. Texture the hands in the same way as for the feet.

HEADS

13 Build up the shape of the face with small pieces of Bridal White sugarpaste and bring out the snout and the eye sockets. Cover the head with 150g (5¼oz) of Mocha Cream sugarpaste and 150g (5¼oz) of Bridal White sugarpaste using the double-sided coating technique (see page 18).

14 Draw a central line down the snout, mark a 'V' shape for the nose and an inverted 'V' to mark the mouth. Add seam lines around the top of the head and around the snout, then texture the paste with a Dresden tool to create a fur effect in the same way as for the bodies.

TOP TIP
Use a real teddy bear as a guide for the fur and facial features.

15 For the nose, roll a small piece of black modelling paste into a 1.5cm (½") diameter ball, then flatten the ball with your fingers and mould it into a triangular shape. Attach the nose to the tip of the snout with a little cooled, boiled water and shape it so it fits inside the marks on the paste. Use a small CelPin to draw lines down the nose to add texture.

16 For the eyes, colour a small amount of leftover sugarpaste with Bulrush paste food colour to make it dark brown. Roll the paste into a 1cm (³/₈") diameter ball, then cut the ball in half with a small palette knife to make two eyes of equal sizes. Stick them into the eye sockets with pre-boiled water. Roll a 4mm (¼") ball of black modelling paste and cut it in half to make two equal-sized pupils. Stick them to the centre of each eye.

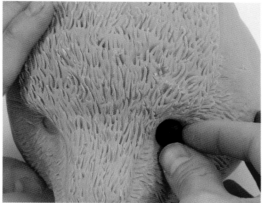

17 To make the ears, roll a piece of Mocha Cream sugarpaste into a 5cm (2") diameter ball, then flatten the ball into oval shape. Press the middle of the paste with your thumb, leaving a rim around the edge. Cut the piece in half to make two symmetrical ears, push them out further with your thumb then stick them onto the top of the head.

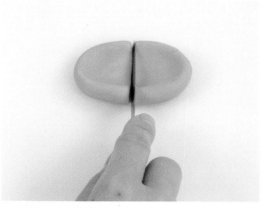

18 Place a 'hidden' pillar over the dowel so it meets the top layer of the body. Cut to size with a craft knife and replace, then stick the head onto the body and secure with a small amount of royal icing.

19 Repeat steps 11–18 for the second teddy bear.

BOW TIE

20 Roll out a strip of black modelling paste to approximately 4cm x 15cm (1½" x 6") in size. Fold both ends inwards so they meet in the middle, then gather the paste together in the centre. Make another smaller strip of black modelling paste and wrap it over the join to make the knot in the bow tie.

26 Use some Edelweiss paste food colour to lighten the area around the mouth and nose and paint on the mouth with Bulrush paste colour and a fine round paintbrush. Cover the eyes with a layer of confectioners' glaze using a round paintbrush.

27 Lightly airbrush each teddy with a mix of Bulrush, Teddy Bear Brown and Marigold liquid food colours.

TOP TIP

To create a glossy effect for the eyes, use multiple coats of confectioners' glaze and allow each layer to dry before you apply the next.

TIARA

21 Roll out some White SFP very thinly and cut out a strip that is approximately 10cm x 20cm (4" x 7¾") in size. Emboss the paste with a textured rolling pin and dust the surface with a little Double Cream lustre dust. Fold the paste in half lengthways with the dusted-side up, then dampen the bottom of the fold with a little cooled, boiled water. Roll the paste up loosely into a basic rolled rose. Make several fabric-effect roses in various sizes.

COLLAR

22 Make a White SFP bow in the same way as for the bow tie and a fabric-effect rose following the step above. Stick the rose to the centre of the bow with a little cooled, boiled water and leave to dry.

TOP HAT

23 Using the crisped rice cereal mix, model a cylinder shape that is approximately 4cm (1½") in diameter and 5cm (2") tall. Push a plastic dowel down the centre of the cylinder, leaving approximately 5cm (2") sticking out. Cut any excess from the end with wire cutters and cover the hat with a thin layer of royal icing. Roll some black modelling paste to approximately 3mm (⅛") thick, cover the top hat then leave it to dry on a block of polystyrene. Mark a line around the hat approximately 1cm (⅜") up from the base.

PAINTING

24 Use some Chestnut paste food colour and a flat paintbrush to paint over the whole of each teddy, giving the fur a richer colour.

25 Brush some Bulrush paste food colour over the seams, eyes, mouth and ears to give them depth.

FINISHING TOUCHES

28 For the brim of the hat, roll a ball of black modelling paste to approximately 5cm (2") in diameter. Flatten it into a circle that is approximately 5mm (¼") thick and fold up the edges to curl the brim. Insert the dowel from the top section of the hat into the brim and down through the head, by the groom's right ear. Secure in place with some royal icing.

29 Stick the collar to the left of the bride's neck using royal icing, then attach the roses to the top of the bride's head as a tiara. Pipe small pearls around the tiara using a no. 2 nozzle and some royal icing. Allow them to dry, then paint the pearls using White Satin lustre dust mixed with a little clear alcohol.

30 Cover the board in sections using Bridal White sugarpaste to create a soft fabric effect (see page 16).

31 Trim the board with ivory ribbon to finish.

SWEETHEART SWANS

I was inspired to create this design after I noticed an elegant swan couple making a heart shape with their necks in the background of my own wedding photos. A great symbol of eternal love, this pair of swans would make the perfect romantic centrepiece for any wedding.

Size: approx. 70cm x 30.5cm x 39cm (27" x 12" x 15") I Serves 90

EDIBLES

2 x 30.5cm (12") square sponge cakes

3 quantities of buttercream (see page 12)

2 quantities of crisped rice cereal mix (see page 12)

SK Sugarpaste (rolled fondant): 3kg (6lb 9¾oz) Bridal White

SK Sugar Florist Paste (SFP, gum paste): 200g (7oz) White

1kg (2lb 3¼oz) SK Instant Mix Royal Icing

SK Professional Paste Food Colours: Marigold (tangerine), Jet Black

SK Designer Bridal Satin Lustre Dust Food Colour: White Satin

SK Professional Liquid Food Colours (for airbrushing): Chestnut (soft beige) (optional)

Modelling paste (sugarpaste + CMC, see page 12): 2kg (4lb 6½oz) Bridal White

Pearl lustre spray (PME) (optional)

EQUIPMENT

Basic equipment (see pages 6–9)

2 x 35.5cm x 61cm (14" x 24") rectangular cake drums (boards), glued together

51cm x 76cm (20" x 30") piece of 5mm (¼") thick foamboard

2 x 1.12m (44") pieces of aluminium wire

Paintbrushes: nos. 1 (fine), 2, 3, 10 (flat) (SK)

Hot glue gun

Satin ribbon: 2m (79") x 25mm (1") width white

Templates and diagram (see pages 134–135)

ARMATURES

1 Use a photocopier to enlarge the swan board templates by 200%. Draw around each template onto a piece of 5mm (¼") foamboard and cut around them with a Stanley knife. Cover each piece of foamboard completely with food sealing wrap.

2 Place the foamboard armatures onto the cake drum and position them so that they are side-by-side, then turn the front of each template in towards the other. The swans should be sitting at an angle across the board so they are leaning into each other (see diagram on page 134). Use a blunt knife to score around the outline of the foamboards onto the cake board. Mark a point just in front of each outline for the neck armatures, then drill two small holes at the marks: the holes must be small enough to hold the aluminium wires securely in place.

3 Fold both pieces of aluminium wire in half and twist the wire together tightly.

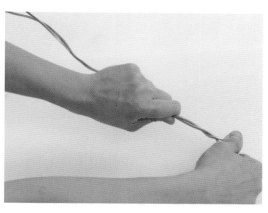

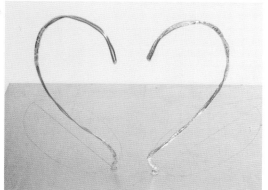

Working back from the fold in the wire which will make the beak, shape the wire into the curve of a swan's neck. Do the same with the second wire, but bend the curve in the opposite way to the first, so that the necks make a heart shape when put together. Wrap both of the wires in cake board foil, push the end of each wire into the holes in the cake drum and secure in place with hot glue from a glue gun. Leave to dry.

MOULDING THE NECK SHAPES

4 Once you have prepared the crisped rice cereal mix, take handfuls of the mix and mould it around the wire armature to fill out the neck. Cover the whole armature with the crisped rice cereal mix, making it thicker towards the base of the neck so it is approximately 4cm (1½") in diameter at the base.

5 When you are happy with the shape, make up some royal icing and use a palette knife to cover the whole neck with icing. Leave the head uncovered. Make the second neck in the same way and allow both to set for 24 hours.

HEADS

6 Use a Dresden tool to mark out the position of the eyes, the beak and the cheeks on each rice cereal mix head. It is a good idea to use a picture of a real swan as reference to achieve the correct proportions for the head.

7 Using the marks as a guide, build up the shape of the head with small pieces of white modelling paste. Take a 2.5cm (1") diameter ball of white modelling paste and mould the paste around the beak. Flatten a similar-sized ball of paste into an oval shape and stick it along the top of the head. Use the same technique to make the cheeks and stick them to either side of the head so that it is completely covered with paste.

8 Draw a line around the edge of the beak and mark on the nostrils with a Dresden tool. Use the smaller end of a bone tool to make indents for the eye sockets.

9 Roll out some white modelling paste to approximately 3mm (1/8") thick and cover the exposed part at the top of the neck. Smooth over any joins on the head with a Dresden tool.

10 Make a ball of Tuxedo Black sugarpaste that is approximately 5mm (1/4") in diameter and cut in half with a small palette knife. Roll each half into a smaller ball and stick one into each eye socket with a little cooled, boiled water.

COVERING THE NECKS

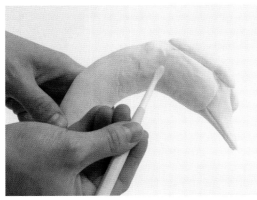

11 Roll out 250g (8¾oz) of Bridal White sugarpaste to approximately 2mm (1/16") thick. Dampen the neck with a little cooled, boiled water, wrap the paste around the armature, then smooth over the join with a Dresden tool. Don't worry if you can't hide the join completely as the feather texture will disguise any imperfections.

12 To add texture, use the pointed end of a Dresden tool to draw short lines (approximately 5mm (1/4") long) along the head and down the neck, but vary the angle of each stroke slightly so that the texture looks natural.

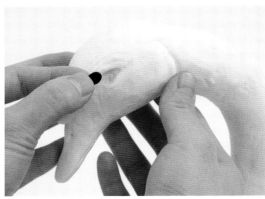

13 Repeat steps 6–12 for the second swan, but make the knob on top of the bill slightly larger than the first to distinguish the male swan from the female.

FEATHERS

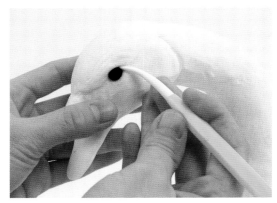

14 Working with a small piece of White SFP at a time, roll out a small circle very thinly and cut out a number of freehand feather shapes from the paste with a cutting wheel. The feather shapes will look more realistic if you cut them out freehand, rather than using a cutter. Vary the size of the feathers so that they are between 2cm and 4cm (¾" and 1½") long.

15 To add detail to each feather, use a Dresden tool to draw lots of small lines from the edge of the feather in towards the centre. Depending on your speed, you can make 5–10 feathers at a time before the paste becomes too dry to add texture. Soften the edge of each feather with your fingers to give it a little movement. Make approximately 50–60 feathers in various sizes and leave them to dry on a piece of food-grade sponge: you may want to make extras in case of breakages.

CARVING THE CAKES

16 Cut one of the 30.5cm (12") square cakes in half, then place the first half of the cake on one of the foamboard armatures for the swan's body. Use a serrated knife to cut off the corners of the second half of cake, then position the second half on top of the first tier so that it sits towards the back.

17 Place one of the leftover corners on top of the cake to create the tail and stick down with a little buttercream. Carve the cakes into the body shape with a serrated knife, following the foamboard as a guide. Round off the edges of the cakes, then trim the front of the cake at an angle to make the front of the body.

18 Once you are happy with the shape, remove the top tier and dowel the first layer of the swan's body (see page 18). Stick the tiers together with a layer of buttercream, crumb-coat the whole cake and leave it to chill in the freezer (if you have room) or a cool place for one hour. Repeat for the second swan.

COVERING THE CAKES

19 Place the first cake on a spare cake board and use small pieces of Bridal White sugarpaste to build up the parts of the cake that need a little support, such as the tail and the wings. Roll out 1kg (2lb 3¼oz) of Bridal White sugarpaste to a thickness of 6mm (5/16") and cover the swan all in one go with the paste.

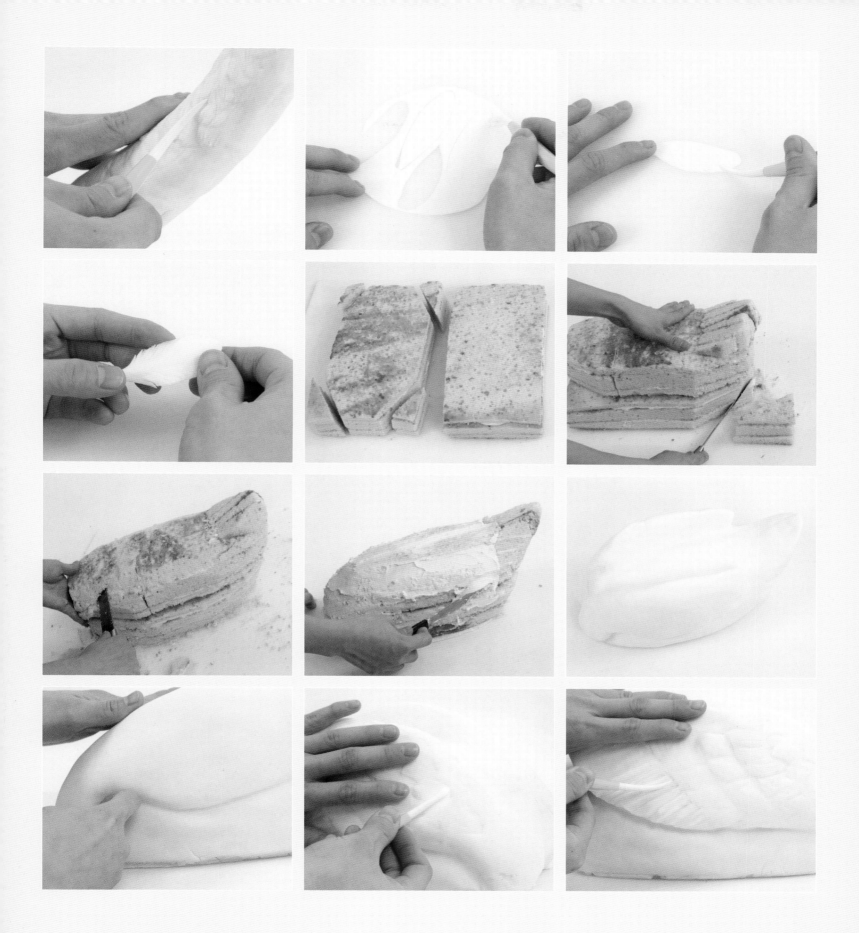

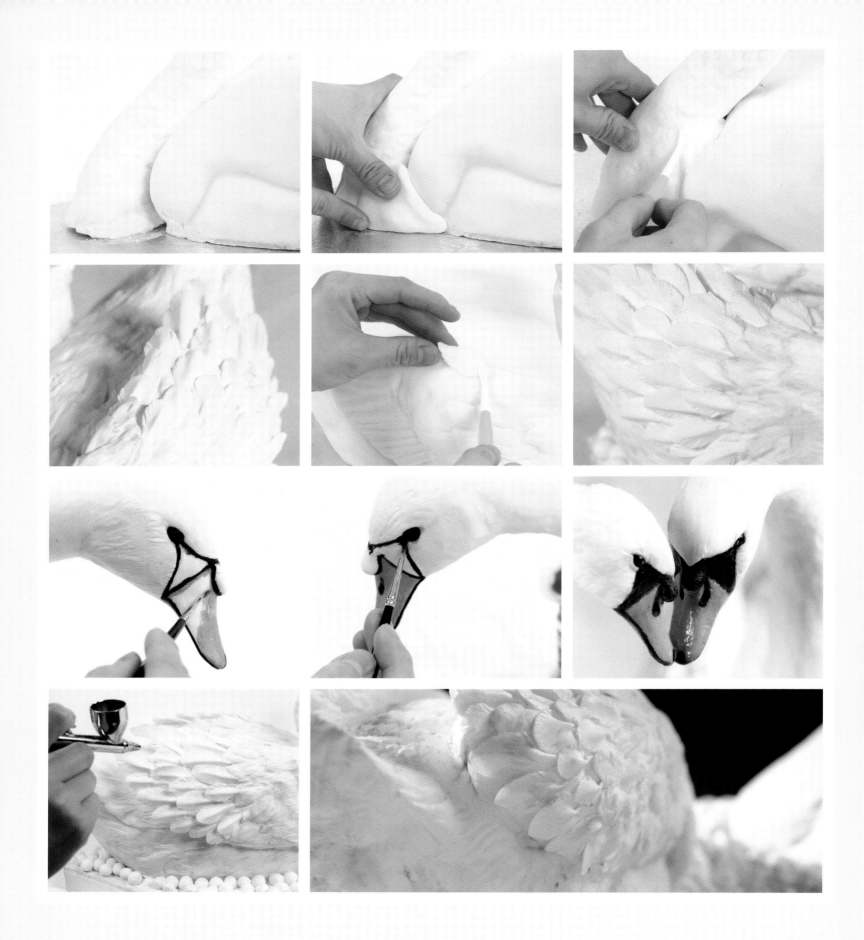

20 Use your hands to model the shape of the wings from the sugarpaste covering. Press the sugarpaste gently all the way from the tip of the wing to the bottom of the neck to define the edge of the wing.

21 Use the pointed end of a Dresden tool to texture the back of the body and the wings: make gentle V-shapes in the paste to represent the shape of a feather, then draw fine lines down the middle of each V-shape. To texture the ends of the wings, draw lines down the paste with a Dresden tool to make them look like longer feathers. The lines should be approximately 7cm (2¾") long at the tip to approximately 3cm (1⅛") long at the base of the wing.

ASSEMBLING THE SWANS

22 Spread some royal icing over one of the outlines that you marked on the cake drum earlier. Carefully use a large palette knife to lift the swan from the spare board and position the front of the cake against the neck. Make sure the body is supporting the neck at the correct angle, then secure in place.

23 Hide the gap between the base of the neck and the body with a piece of white modelling paste and use a Dresden tool to smooth over the join. Texture the bottom of the neck and the front of the body using the same technique as for the neck (see steps 12 and 13).

24 Starting from the tip and moving down towards the middle of the wing, carefully attach the feathers one-by-one with a little cooled, boiled water, then use a Dresden tool to blend the end of each feather into the body.

25 Repeat steps 19–24 for the second swan.

PAINTING THE HEADS

26 Use some Jet Black paste food colour and a no. 1 round paintbrush to draw lines from the corner of the eye to the bottom and top of the beak.

27 Dilute a little Marigold paste food colour with a little cooled, boiled water and paint around the outline of the bill with a no. 2 round paintbrush, then fill it in with the orange colour.

28 Dilute some Jet Black paste food colour with a little cooled, boiled water and a no. 2 round paintbrush to fill in the black areas on the face. Leave to dry.

29 Paint the eyes and the beak with confectioners' glaze and a no. 3 round paintbrush to give them a glossy effect.

FINISHING TOUCHES

30 To add shading, airbrush the deep creases in the body, such as the wing joints, the back and the areas under the wings with Chestnut airbrush colour to make an ivory shade.

31 To decorate the cake board, roll approximately 300 balls from 5mm (¼") to 1cm (⅜") in diameter from white modelling paste then leave them to dry.

32 Tip some White Satin lustre dust into a small pot, place a few balls in the pot at a time and shake it to cover them with dust and give them a pearlescent sheen. Take them out and remove the excess dust with a dusting brush. Repeat to coat all the remaining balls of paste.

33 Spread a thin layer of royal icing over the cake board and stick the pearls all over it. Spray lightly with the pearl lustre spray if you wish to add more sheen.

34 Trim the board with white satin ribbon to finish.

Sweetheart Swans

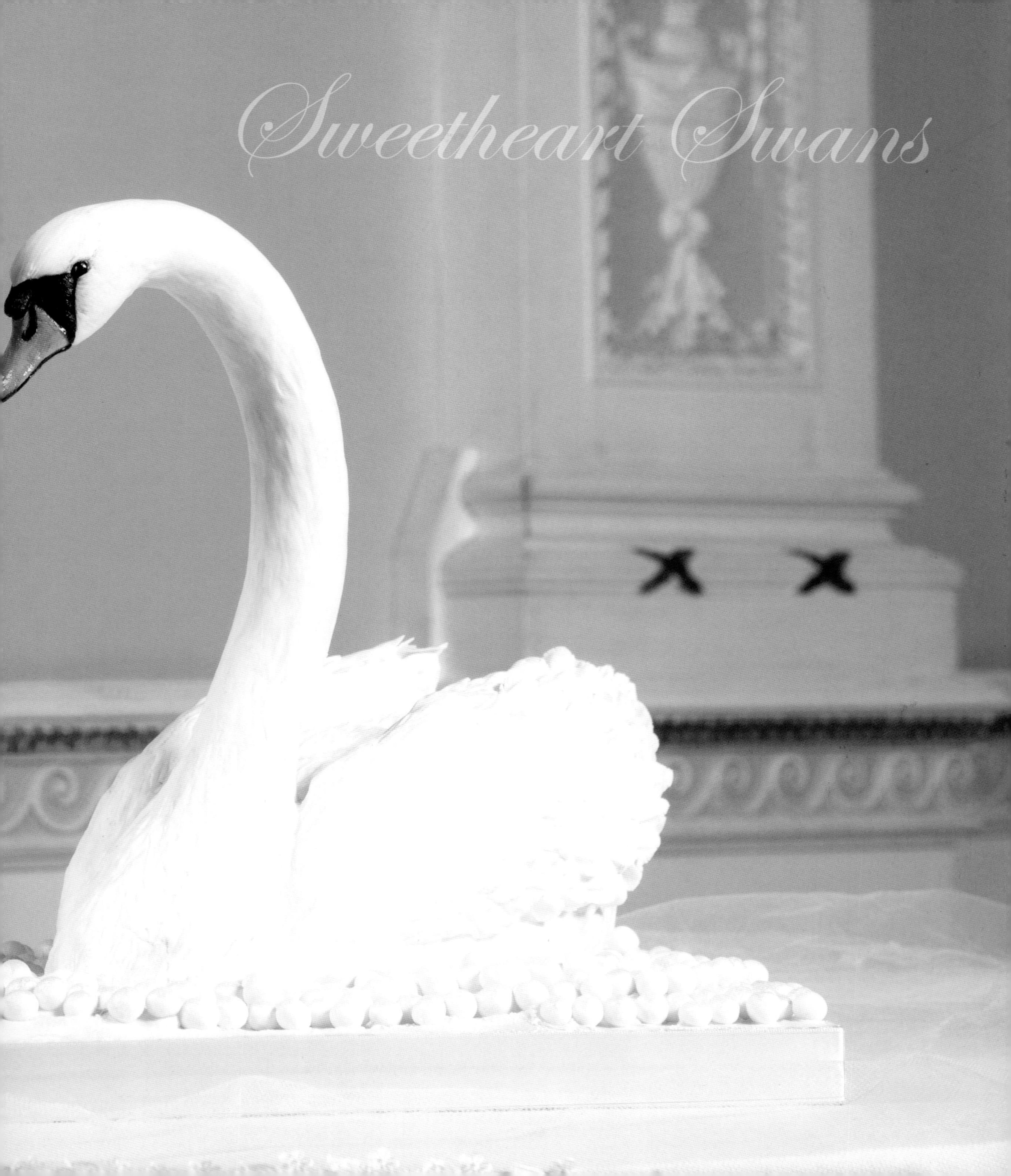

BALLOON RIDE

Romantic hot air balloon rides are a popular choice for those wanting to pop the question – this personalised cake design is guaranteed to put the happy couple on cloud nine.

Size approx. 25.5cm x 25.5cm x 40.5cm (10" x 10" x 16") | Serves 100

EDIBLES

3 x 25.5cm (10") round sponge cakes

4 quantities of buttercream (see page 12)

SK Sugarpaste (rolled fondant): 1kg (2lb 3¼oz) Ballerina Pink, 500g (1lb 1¾oz) Bridal White, 1kg (2lb ¾oz) Vintage Pink

SK Sugar Florist Paste (SFP, gum paste): 150g (5¼oz) White

Modelling paste (sugarpaste + CMC, see page 12): 200g (7oz) Bridal White, 100g (3½oz) Bridal White with a touch of Chestnut paste food colour, 100g (3½oz) Bridal White with a touch of Bulrush paste food colour, 50g (1¾oz) Tuxedo Black

200g (7oz) SK Instant Mix Royal Icing

SK Professional Paste Food Colours: Berberis, Bulrush (dark brown), Chestnut (soft beige), Edelweiss (white), Jet Black, Sunflower

SK Quality Food Colour (QFC) Pastes: Black, Blue, Brown, Pink

SK Professional Liquid Food Colours (for airbrushing): Fuchsia

EQUIPMENT

Basic equipment (see pages 6–9)

35.5cm (14") square piece of chipboard, wrapped in cake board foil

18cm (7") round polystyrene dummy

18cm, 20.5cm and 23cm (7", 8" and 9") circles cut out of 5mm (¼") thick foamboard, covered with food sealing wrap

18cm, 23cm and 25.5cm (7", 9" and 10") round cake drums (boards)

40.5cm long x 18mm diameter (16" x ¾") wooden dowel, wrapped in cake board foil

10cm long x 4cm diameter (4" x 1½") PVC pipe, covered with food sealing wrap

Electric drill with 18mm (¾") drill bit

18mm (¾") diameter wooden stake

Hot glue gun

Hidden pillar (Wilton)

Basketweave embosser (PC)

Rose petal cutters, set of 5 (FMM)

4cm (1½") SK Great Impressions Petal Veiner: Tea Rose

Food-grade foam pad

Round cutters: 4cm, 7.5cm (1½", 3")

Fine paintbrush (SK)

Satin ribbons: 1.47m (58") x 25mm (1") width white, 1m (40") x 3mm (⅛") width white

Template (see page 133)

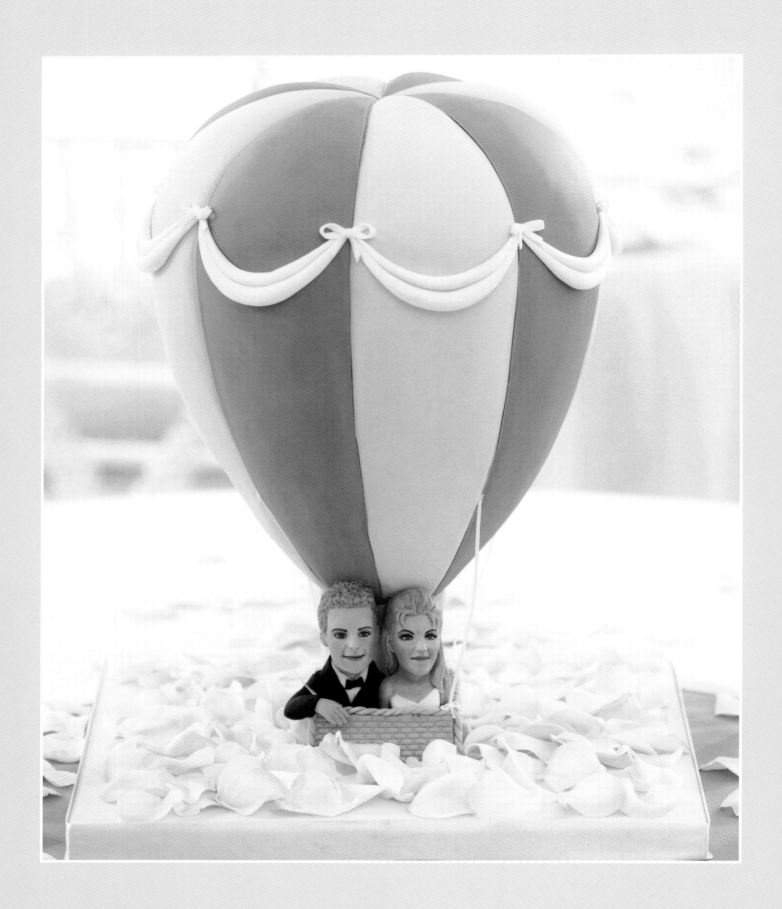

ARMATURES

1   To make the divider template, draw around an 18cm (7") cake board onto a piece of greaseproof paper and cut it out with scissors. Fold it in half three times to divide the circle into eight equal segments.

2   Draw a 7.5cm (3") diameter circle on the top and in the centre of the round polystyrene dummy. Make a hole in the centre of the dummy with a pointed wooden stake: the hole should be big enough for the 18mm (¾") diameter wooden dowel to fit through. Still using the hot wire cutter, cut from the top edge of the dummy down to the marked circle on the bottom. Cut into the sides of the dummy at an angle so that you are left with a flat-bottomed vase shape. Cover the polystyrene armature with food sealing wrap, then cover with a thin layer of Bridal White sugarpaste and leave to dry for 24 hours (follow the cake covering steps on page 17).

3   Roll out some white modelling paste to approximately 1cm (³⁄₈") thick and cut out a circle with the 7.5cm (3") round cutter. Cut out a smaller hole from the middle of the paste with a 4cm (1½") round cutter and stick the ring of paste onto the smaller end of the polystyrene armature.

4   Cover the square chipboard in cake board foil, then use an electric drill with an 18mm (¾") drill bit to make a hole through the centre. Cover the hole with a piece of strong tape underneath the board, then cover the top of the board with a thin layer of white sugarpaste (see page 16). Cut away the sugarpaste covering the hole in the board, then leave to dry for 24 hours. Once dry, wrap the wooden dowel in cake board foil and hammer it into the hole in the top of the board, ensuring it fits securely in place.

5   Wrap the PVC pipe in food sealing wrap so it is completely covered. Roll out a 10cm (4") wide strip of white sugarpaste that is approximately 8mm (³⁄₈") thick, cover the pipe with the paste and leave to dry. Place the coated pipe down the dowel and secure it to the board

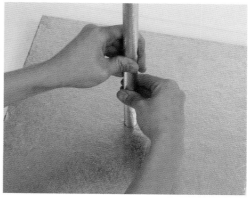
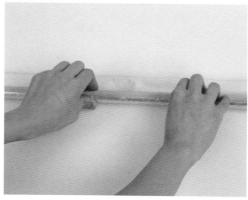

with a little royal icing. Push the polystyrene armature (with the smaller side facing down) down the dowel so that it sits on top of the pipe. Secure it to the pipe with a small amount of royal icing.

6   Cover the circles of foamboard completely with food sealing wrap, then use the wooden stake to make a hole in the centre of each one. The final assembled armature should look like the picture (right).

CARVING THE CAKES

7   For the bottom tier, place an 18cm (7") cake board centrally on top of the first 25.5cm (10") round cake and slide a 23cm (9") covered, round foamboard underneath the cake. Use a large, serrated knife to carve away the cake between the top and bottom boards, giving the sides of the cake a gentle curve. Remove both boards once you have finished. Place the 18cm (7") round foamboard on top of

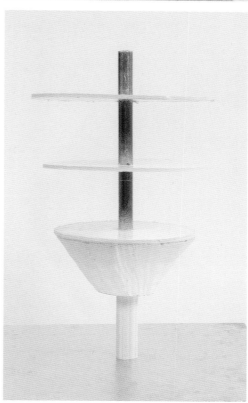

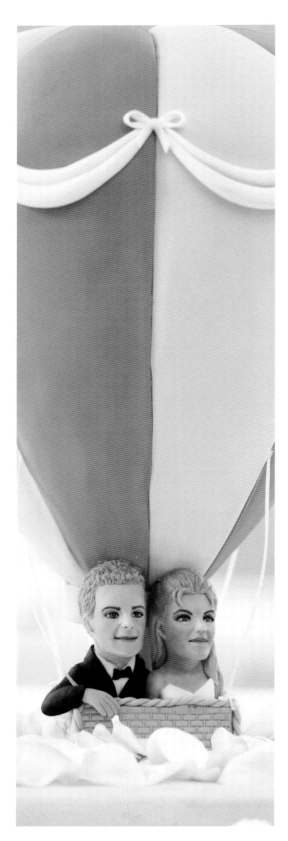

the cake and flip the cake over so that it is sitting on the board. Position the divider template on top of the cake and use the back of a knife to make marks at the end of each fold line. Crumb-coat the sides of the cake.

8   For the middle tier, use the same method as described in step 7 but place a 23cm (9") cake board on top of a second 25.5cm (10") round cake and a 25.5cm (10") round board underneath it. Carve away the cake between the boards and mark out the sections as before, then remove both boards. Put the 20.5cm (8") round foamboard on top of the cake and flip it over. Crumb-coat the sides of the cake.

9   For the top tier, use the back of a knife and the template to mark the cake at the end of each fold line and at the central point. Remove the template and use a knife to gently draw lines between the marks, dividing the cake into eight equal sections. Round off the edges of the cake to create a shallow dome, leaving the very top of the cake flat. Carve into each line to make the sections more prominent.

10   Dowel each tier (see page 18) and push a 'hidden' pillar into the centre to make a hole for the armature to go through. Stack the cakes to make the balloon shape, making sure to line up the indents on the side of the cake, and secure each layer with buttercream. Continue carving into the lines all the way down the cake: it is a good idea to use a smoother as a guide to make sure each line is straight. Crumb-coat the cake once again to seal the joins between tiers. Leave the cake to firm up in the freezer before putting it on the armature.

11   Spread some royal icing over the top of the polystyrene armature and assemble the whole cake while it is still frozen. The assembled cake should look like the picture opposite.

COVERING THE BALLOON

12   Dampen the first section of the balloon with a little cooled, boiled water to make it sticky. Roll out some Ballerina Pink sugarpaste

to approximately 2mm (¹⁄₁₆") thick and large enough so it completely covers one section of the balloon. Working from top to bottom, stick the paste onto the balloon and smooth down with a smoother. Trim away any excess paste with a small palette knife.

13   Working your way around the balloon in a clockwise direction, cover the next section with Vintage Pink sugarpaste in the same way. Before you attach the paste, use a pizza wheel to cut one side of the paste straight, then position the straight side as closely as possible beside the first section. Continue in this way until the balloon is completely covered.

SWAGS

14   Insert eight cocktail sticks evenly around the cake: place them in between each sugarpaste section approximately ¼ of the way down the balloon. Carefully mark a curved line for each of the swags with a modelling tool, then remove all the cocktail sticks once you have finished marking out the swags.

15   Roll out a long sausage of Bridal White sugarpaste that is approximately 1cm (³⁄₈") in diameter. Cut the sausage of paste into eight 3cm (1¹⁄₈") pieces, then roll out and taper the ends of each sausage to make them long enough to fit across one section of the balloon. Use a little cooled, boiled water to stick each swag in place following the marks in the paste.

16   Repeat to make smaller swags that are approximately 6mm (¼") in diameter and attach these above the thicker swags.

BOWS

17   Roll out some White SFP thinly and cut out eight strips that are 5mm wide x 2cm long (¼" x ¾") with a cutting wheel. Take the ends of each strip, fold them into the middle to make bow loops and pinch the join. Make nine more strips that are 5mm wide x 4cm long (¼" x 1½") and cut the end of each strip at an

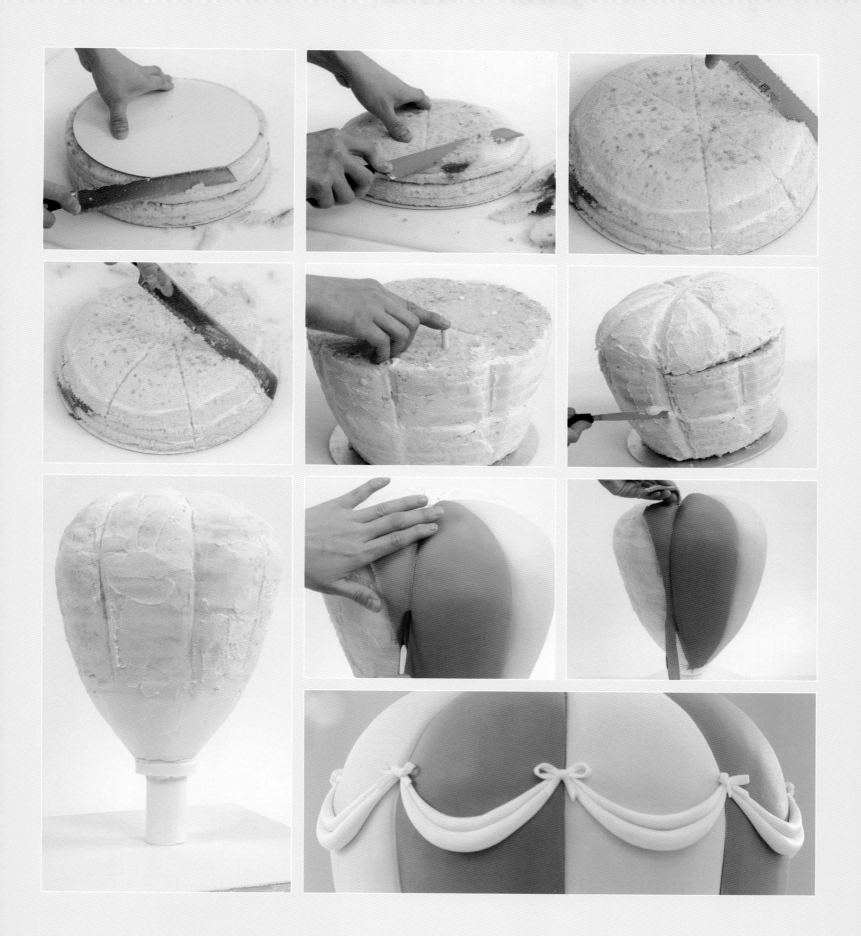

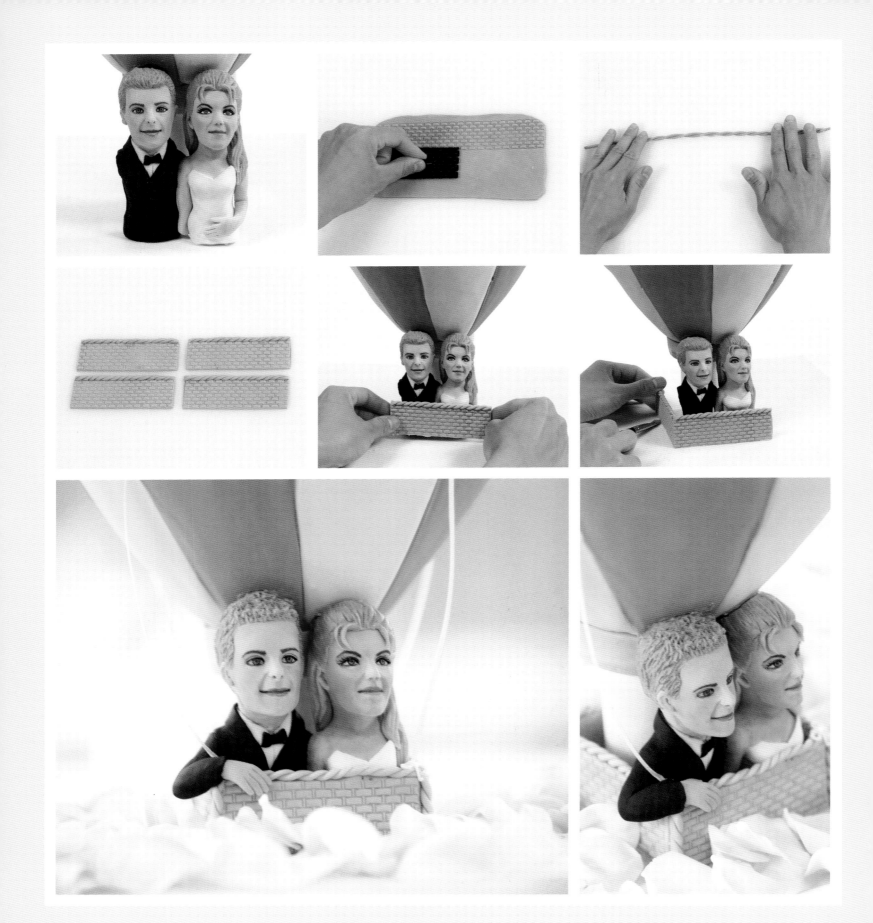

angle to make the bow tails. Stick two bow tails to the middle of each bow. Make the knots for each bow from the remaining strip of SFP. Stick the bows between the swags with a dab of cooled, boiled water.

BRIDE AND GROOM

18 Make the heads and torsos for the bride and groom following the instructions on pages 36–39. Make the bride's arms using Chestnut-coloured modelling paste (see page 42); you do not need to make the hand for the right arm as this will not be visible. For the bride's hair, colour some white modelling paste with Sunflower paste food colour, roll out a thin sausage that is 2.5cm (1") long and taper at one end. Texture it lightly using a Dresden tool. Attach it to the base of the head and texture to disguise the join. Repeat the process until the back of the head is covered.

19 For the top of the head, make a 1.5cm (5/8") ball of the Sunflower-coloured paste. Flatten it out and attach it over the top of the head, shaping it around the face to create the hairline. Texture it using a Dresden tool and attach some smaller strands at the front to make the fringe.

20 Make the groom's right arm from black modelling paste but do not attach it at this stage. Make the groom's hair from Berberis-coloured modelling paste following the instructions on page 39. The lower part of the bodies aren't needed for this project as they are hidden by the basket.

21 Decide which side will be the front of the balloon and stick the figurines side-by-side tightly against the central dowel with royal icing.

BASKET

22 Roll out a small amount of dark brown modelling paste and cut out a rectangle that is approximately 5cm x 20.5cm (2" x 8") in size. Texture the paste with the basketweave embosser and cut the paste into quarters to make four panels that are approximately 2.5cm x 10cm (1"x 4") in size. Leave them to dry completely.

23 Roll out a sausage of dark brown modelling paste very thinly to approximately 25.5cm (10") long. Fold the sausage in half and twist the ends together to make a rope. Dampen the edges of the basket with a little cooled, boiled water and attach a piece of rope across the top of each basket panel. Trim to size.

24 Position the first panel as closely as possible in front of the models and stick to the board with royal icing. Stick the remaining three basket panels around the base of the balloon with royal icing and neaten the edges with a damp paintbrush. Make more lengths of rope in the same way as before and stick them down the corners of the basket to hide the joins.

25 Cut the narrow white ribbon into four lengths that are long enough to reach from the bottom of the balloon to the corners of the basket. Use royal icing to stick one end to the balloon and one end to each of the corners of the basket.

26 Attach the groom's right arm in place with cooled, boiled water once you've assembled the basket.

FINISHING TOUCHES

27 Roll out some White SFP very thinly and use the small and medium-sized rose petal cutters to cut out approximately 50 petals. Place each petal on a foam pad and soften the edges with a ball tool. Vein each petal with the rose petal veiner and leave them to dry on a piece of scrunched-up kitchen paper. To colour, use an airbrush to spray each petal lightly with Fuchsia liquid food colour. Scatter the petals around the board.

28 Trim the edge of the board with white ribbon to finish.

Balloon Ride

FOUNTAIN OF ETERNAL LOVE

I adapted this cake design from an ornate, Renaissance-style fountain I fell in love with in Italy. Symbolic of eternity, this impressive fountain would make a spectacular centrepiece in any wedding venue.

Size approx. 30.5cm x 30.5cm x 58cm (12" x 12" x 23") | Serves 85

EDIBLES

20.5cm and 30.5cm (8" and 12") round sponge cakes

2 quantities of buttercream (see page 12)

1 quantity of crisped rice cereal mix (see page 12)

SK Sugarpaste (rolled fondant): 2.5kg (5lb 8¼oz) Bridal White

Modelling paste (sugarpaste + CMC, see page 12): 1.5kg (3lb 5oz) Bridal White

700g (1lb 8¾oz) SK Instant Mix Royal Icing

SK Professional Paste Food Colours: Bulrush (dark brown), Cyclamen (ruby), Edelweiss (white)

SK Professional Liquid Food Colours (for airbrushing): Blackberry (black), Bulrush (dark brown), Daffodil (yellow), Leaf Green

Clear alcohol, e.g. vodka or gin

EQUIPMENT

Basic equipment (see pages 6–9)

15cm and 25.5cm (6" and 10") circles cut out of 10mm (³/₈") thick foamboard

35.5cm (14") square piece of chipboard, wrapped in cake board foil

10cm and 20.5cm (4" and 8") spare round cake boards

3 x pieces of PVC water pipe: 16.5cm long x 4cm diameter (6½" x 1½"), 11.5cm long x 4cm diameter (4½" x 1½") and 12.5cm x 1.8cm diameter (5"x ¾")

48cm long x 1.8cm diameter (19" x ½") wooden dowel, wrapped in cake board foil

Hidden pillar (Wilton)

Electric drill fitted with 18mm (¾") drill bit

Polystyrene block

Small food-grade sponge

Satin ribbon: 1.48m (58") x 25mm (1") width ivory

Templates and diagram (see page 136)

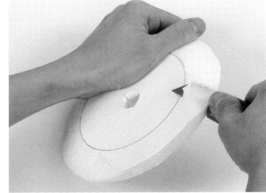

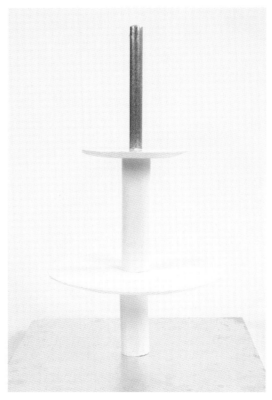

ARMATURES

1 Make a photocopy of the fountain template on page 136.

2 Draw around a 20.5cm (8") round cake drum onto a piece of greaseproof paper and cut out with scissors. Fold the circle in half four times so that you divide it into 16 equal sections. Write the number '16' on the circle: this will be used as a template to mark out the 30.5cm (12") round cake. Cut out a second circle and fold in half twice, then fold it into thirds to make 12 equal sections. Write the number '12' on the circle: this will be used as a template for the 20.5cm (8") round cake.

3 Place a 10cm (4") round cake drum in the middle of the 15cm (6") round foamboard and draw around it. Repeat with the 20.5cm (8") round cake board on the 25.5cm (10") round foamboard. Make a hole in the centre of both pieces of foamboard

with a pointed wooden stake. Use a Stanley knife to taper the edges of both foamboards: cut the board at an angle between the outline of the circle and the edge of the foamboard, making the board narrower at the edge. Clear away all the trimmings then wrap both pieces of foamboard in food sealing wrap so that they are completely covered.

4 Mark the central point on the square chipboard, then drill a hole at the mark using an 18mm (¾") drill bit. Cover the board completely with cake board foil.

5 Cover the wooden dowel in cake board foil and secure the dowel in the hole in the board using hot glue from a glue gun. Hammer the dowel into place to make sure that it fits firmly in the hole and leave to dry in place. Check that all the pieces for the armature fit over the central dowel, then take them off again before making the cake.

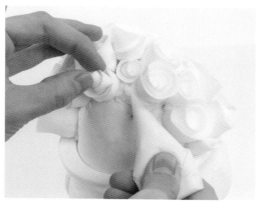

6   Roll out some Bridal White sugarpaste to approximately 3mm (1/8") thick and until the paste is large enough to cover the board. Cut a hole in the centre, carefully lift the paste over the central post then cover the top of the board with the paste. Roll out some more white sugarpaste to approximately 3mm (1/8") thick and cut out rectangles of paste large enough to wrap around each piece of PVC pipe. Cover each pipe with the paste and stick down with a little cooled, boiled water. Leave the covered board and all the covered pipes to dry for at least 24 hours.

VASE

7   Mould some of the crisped rice cereal mix into a cone that is 12.5cm (5") tall with a base that is approximately 10cm (4") in diameter. Push the 12.5cm (5") pipe into the base of the cone, leaving approximately 7.5cm (3") of the pipe protruding from the bottom. The total height of the vase armature should be 20.5cm (8") overall. Leave to firm.

8   Once it has firmed up, use a palette knife to cover the vase with a thin layer of soft-peak royal icing to create a smooth surface. Leave the vase to dry for another 24 hours.

9   Roll out a thin layer of white sugarpaste and cover the vase with the paste to create a base coat. Following the diagram as a guide, use a sterilised ruler to mark out the sections of the vase (see page 136). To build up the shape, attach thicker pieces of white sugarpaste to each section you have marked out on the armature.

10   To finish the vase, make several thin strips of white modelling paste that are pointed at one end. Starting from the pointed end, roll up each strip to create a basic rolled rose. Make approximately 50 roses in various sizes and leave them to dry for 24 hours. Once dry, arrange the roses on top of the vase and stick them in place with royal icing.

11   To texture the vase, put some royal icing that is the consistency of thick cream in a paint palette. Dab a small piece of clean, dry, food-grade sponge into the icing then onto a spare board to test the texture before you use it on the vase. You can achieve a different texture by adjusting the consistency of the royal icing: the runnier the consistency, the smoother the texture. Use the sponge to texture the whole vase with a stippled, stone effect and leave to dry.

TOP TIP

Another way of adding texture is to press a new, clean pot scourer onto the surface of soft sugarpaste.

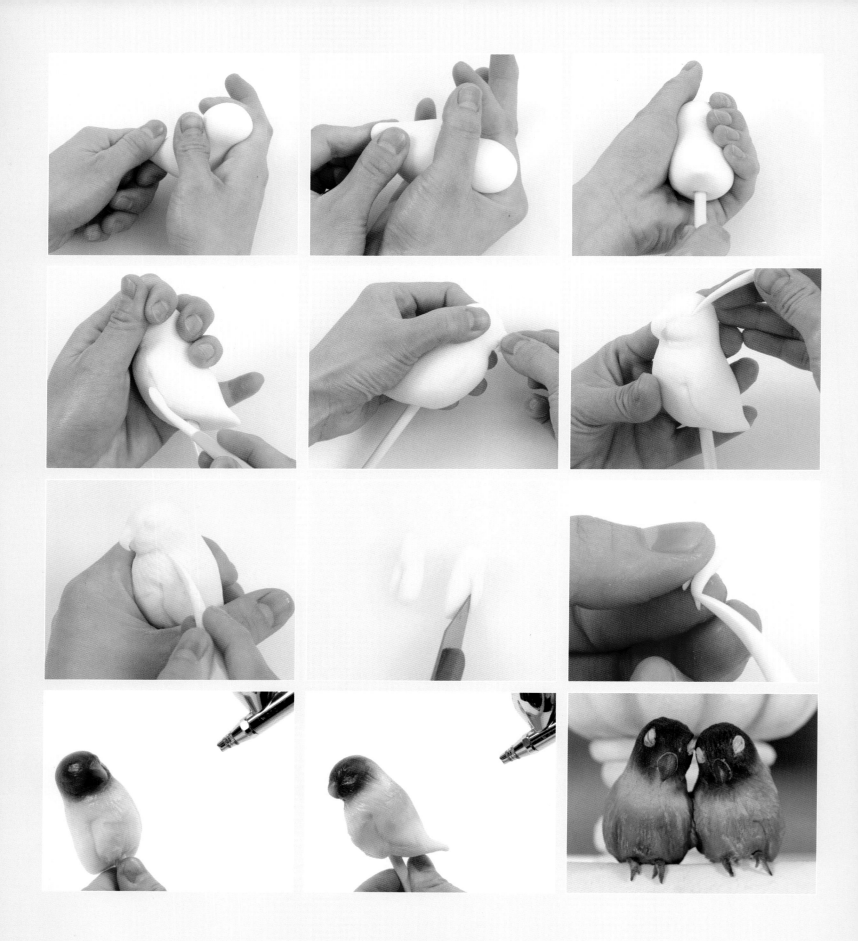

LOVEBIRDS

12 To make a lovebird, model a ball of white modelling paste measuring approximately 6.5cm (2½") in diameter. Elongate the ball slightly to make a wide sausage shape then measure approximately ⅓ of the way down the from the top and use your fingers to bring out the bird's neck. Pinch out the head shape and the tail and use your hands to give the body a little more shape. Insert a plastic cake dowel into the bottom of the bird as a support.

13 Use a Dresden tool to outline the wings and pinch out the very front of the head to make a thin, hooked beak. Mark out the eyes and the eye sockets with a Dresden tool, then use the sharper end of the tool to draw a thin line across the eyelids. Use the same end to draw small lines over the whole body to create a feathered texture (see page 83). Insert the dowel into a block of polystyrene and leave to dry.

14 Roll a small sausage of white modelling paste to approximately 3mm (⅛") thick, then use a craft knife to cut the sausage in half for the two feet. Make a cut halfway along the middle of each foot to make two toes, then gently pull the toes apart and pinch the ends into pointed claws. Draw a line across the toes to mark out the claws, then leave them to dry.

15 Repeat steps 12–14 the make the second lovebird.

16 Start airbrushing the head with Bulrush (dark brown) liquid colour and gradually change the colour to Daffodil. Spray the bottom half of the body in Leaf Green. Using a fine paintbrush, paint the beak

with Cyclamen paste food colour, then paint the feet with Bulrush paste colour and the eyes with Edelweiss paste colour. Use the Edelweiss paste to add some white highlights to the body and beak. Once the body is dry, attach the feet to the bottom of the body with a little royal icing.

CAKES

17 Layer and fill both the 20.5cm and 30.5cm (8" and 12") sponge cakes with buttercream (see page 14), then leave them to chill in the freezer for at least an hour so that the sponge firms up before carving.

18 Place a spare cake board on a turntable, then place the 30.5cm (12") round cake on the board with the flatter side of the cake facing down (this will become the top later on). Position the 25.5cm (10") tapered foamboard on the middle of the cake and start carving around the edge of the cake to create a curved bowl shape. Turn the cake up the right way and check that the shape of the bowl is even. Carve the 20.5cm (8") cake in the same way using the 15cm (6") round foamboard.

19 Once you are happy with the shapes, crumb-coat both cakes then make a hole in the centre of the 30.5cm (12") cake with the covered pipe. This will reduce the amount of crumbs when you insert the cake down the pole later. Return the cakes to the freezer to firm for an hour.

20 Roll out some Bridal White sugarpaste to approximately 5mm (¼") thick and cover both the cakes. Place the '12' template on the 20.5cm (8") cake and the '16' template on the 30.5cm (12") cake and mark out equal sections around the edge of each one.

TOP TIP

By changing the colouring on the birds you can make them into doves or the couple's favourite garden birds; robins would be perfect for a winter wedding.

ASSEMBLY

21 To assemble the cakes, firstly place the 11.5cm (4½") pipe over the dowel and stick it to the board with a little royal icing. Next, place the 30.5cm (12") cake onto the dowel so it sits on top of the first pipe and secure with royal icing. Position the 16.5cm (6½") pipe on top of the first cake and secure. Finally, place the 12.5cm (8") cake on top of the second pillar and secure. The assembled cakes should look like the picture opposite (top left). Insert a 'hidden' pillar into the top cake to support the vase which you will attach later.

22 Following the sections marked on the cakes, draw the dividing lines down the sides of the cake with a sterilised ruler. Gently press your hand into the dividing lines to make each section of the bowl more rounded.

23 To make the decorative borders around the fountain pipe, use the profile template to measure the size of each border, then roll a sausage of white modelling paste that is long enough to fit around the pipe. Flatten the paste with a cake smoother so that you have a strip that is approximately 1.5cm (½") thick, then use the smoother to make one side even thinner to approximately 5mm (¼") thick. Use a pizza wheel to trim the strip to 2.5cm (1") wide and attach it around the base of the fountain with a little cooled, boiled water. Repeat to create another border that is 1.5cm (½") thick and attach it around the very top of the fountain pipe.

24 Roll another strip of white modelling paste that is approximately 1.5cm (½") thick and long enough to fit around the central pipe. Press a small rolling pin into the paste to create a dip along the middle. Trim away the excess paste either side of the dip so that the strip is approximately 5cm (2") wide. Attach it around the middle of the pipe so it sits in between the top and bottom borders.

25 Model a 2cm (¾") diameter ball of white modelling paste into a teardrop shape. Check the size following the profile template and stick it to the bottom of the middle border with a little cooled, boiled water, so they sit at the base. Repeat to make enough teardrops around the pipe, then create the same decoration for the bottom pipe.

26 To create the lip of the fountain roll a 1.5cm (½") thick strip of white modelling paste that is long enough to fit around the edge of the 30.5cm (12") cake. Taper the paste to 5mm (¼") thick on one side in the same way as for the pipe border. Use a pizza wheel and a ruler to trim the long sides of the paste to make the strip approximately 2cm (¾") wide. Attach it around the top edge of the 30.5cm (12") cake with a little cooled, boiled water with the thinner side on the outside. Repeat to make the lip of the fountain for the smaller cake.

27 Texture the whole fountain, including the board, in the same way as for the vase. For the mosaic effect on the board, scratch some random lines into the paste using a veining tool to make it look like pieces of broken tile. Place the vase on top of the fountain and secure with royal icing.

28 Make a light grey airbrush colour by diluting Blackberry liquid food colour with a few drops of clear alcohol. Airbrush the grey colour over deeper creases of the fountain to add shading and give depth to the cake.

29 Attach the two lovebirds to the lip of the top tier with royal icing and position the birds so they are leaning in towards each other.

30 To finish, trim the edge of the board with white satin ribbon and secure in place with a little royal icing.

Fountain of Eternal Love

INDIAN WEDDING ELEPHANT

Indian weddings are usually lavish affairs and a decorated elephant is a traditional way for the groom and his party to make a grand entrance. Capturing the very essence of this majestic creature, this stunning centrepiece is sure to turn heads at any ceremony.

Size: approx. 51cm x 20.5cm x 40.5cm (20" x 8" x 16") | Serves 100

EDIBLES

2 x 30.5cm (12") square sponge cakes

3 quantities of buttercream (see page 12)

4 quantities of crisped rice cereal mix (see page 12)

SK Sugarpaste (rolled fondant): 5kg (11lb ¼oz) Bridal White, 750g (1lb 10½oz) Glamour Red, 250g (8¾oz) Tuxedo Black

1kg (2lb 3¼oz) SK Instant Mix Royal Icing

2kg (4lb 6½oz) SK Pastillage Powder

SK Professional Paste Food Colours: Jet Black, Poinsettia (Christmas red)

SK Professional Dust Food Colours: Bulrush (dark brown), Chestnut (soft beige) (optional)

SK Designer Metallic Lustre Dust Food Colour: Antique Gold

SK Professional Liquid Food Colours (for airbrushing): Bulrush (dark brown), Marigold (tangerine)

SK Confectioners' Glaze

EQUIPMENT

Basic equipment (see pages 6–9)

2 x 35.5cm x 61cm (14"x 24") rectangular cake drums (boards), glued together

51cm x 76cm (20" x 30") pieces of 5mm (¼") and 10mm (³/₈") thick foamboard

40.5cm (16") square piece of 3mm (¹/₈") thick hardboard

4 x 23cm long x 1.8cm diameter (9" x ³/₈") wooden dowels

Electric drill with 2mm (¹/₁₆") drill bit

71cm (28") length of aluminium wire

Piping nozzles: 2 x no. 1

4 plastic cake dowels

Satin ribbon: 2m (79") x 25mm (1") width gold

Templates and diagrams (see pages 137–139)

ARMATURES

1 Use a photocopier to enlarge all the templates by 300% and cut them out. Trace all of the templates onto paper and cut them out.

2 Draw around template B onto the hardboard and cut out the shape with a hacksaw. Drill a hole with a 2mm (^{1}/₁₆") drill bit at each of the marks shown on the template and cover the board completely with cake board foil.

3 Place template C on the 10mm (^{3}/₈") foamboard, draw around it twice to make a piece for the bottom and top layers, then cut them both out with a craft knife. Cover completely with food sealing wrap.

4 Cut out template A from the 5mm (¼") foamboard, then cover completely with food sealing wrap.

5 Drill a hole in both ends of the wooden dowels using a 2mm (^{1}/₁₆") drill bit. Cover each of the dowels completely with cake board foil.

6 Following diagram A, position template B on the cake board to mark where the four leg supports will be positioned then drill a hole at each of the marks using a 2mm (^{1}/₁₆") drill bit. Cover the cake drum with Bridal White sugarpaste (see page 16) then cut away the sugarpaste covering the holes: you should be able to feel the holes through the thin coating of paste. Allow the board to dry completely.

7 Screw each leg dowel in position on the board then place the wooden board on top of them, making sure that the holes line up. Screw the board on top of the dowels, ensuring that the screws are fixed tightly in place.

8 For the trunk, fold the aluminium wire in half and twist the ends together. Bend the twisted wire into an 'S' shape and stick one end of the wire to the front of the wooden board with strong tape: make sure that the wire is stuck firmly in place. The elephant armature should look like the picture above.

NOTE: Remember that it is important to ensure that the cake never comes into direct contact with inedible materials, such as screws and foamboard, as they will contaminate the cake (see page 13). It is best to remove the cake from the armature before you serve it.

STOMACH

9 Turn the 5mm (¼") thick piece of foamboard over and spread a little royal icing over it. Build up the shape of the elephant's stomach with crisped rice cereal mix on top of the board. Make a dome shape that is approximately 5cm (2") deep at the centre: the flat side of the board will be attached under the armature later. Leave four small gaps at the edges of the stomach where the legs will sit, so you can slide the stomach under the main armature. Spread some royal icing over the crisped rice cereal mix to give it a smooth finish.

10 Roll out some Bridal White sugarpaste to approximately 5mm (¹/₄") thick so that it is large enough to cover the stomach section all in one go. Cover the shape, then texture the stomach using a Dresden tool. For softer wrinkles, use the flatter end of the Dresden tool and hold the tool horizontally to create the roughness of the elephant's skin. For fine wrinkles, use the pointed end and draw fine lines using gentle pressure. Allow to dry.

11 Turn the stomach section over and spread a layer of royal icing over the exposed board. Tilt the stomach to fit it in between the legs and secure to the hardboard armature. The stomach should fit snugly between the legs to help hold it in place. Turn the whole armature over and allow the royal icing to dry.

LEGS

12 Working on the armature whilst it is still upturned, cover the legs with a layer of royal icing to help the crisped rice cereal mix stick, then build up the shape of each leg around the armatures. Make the top of the leg wider than the base (up to 4cm (1½") thick). Once you are happy with the shape, use a palette knife to cover the legs with a layer of royal icing to create a smooth surface and leave to dry.

13 Make up some pastillage following the instructions on the pack. Turn the armature up the right way then use balls of pastillage that are approximately 2cm (¾") in diameter to build up the shape of each toe at the base of the legs. Each foot should have four toes.

14 Roll out some pastillage to approximately 3mm (¹/₈") thick and cover the legs with small pieces of the paste. Use the pointed end of a Dresden tool to mark out the separate toes and draw on the nails. Work on one leg at a time so you have enough time to sculpt the pastillage before it dries out. Once you are happy with the shape, texture it using the same technique as for the stomach. Seal the remaining pastillage in an airtight container to keep it soft.

TOP TIP

Use pictures of elephants as a reference to help you make the cake look realistic.

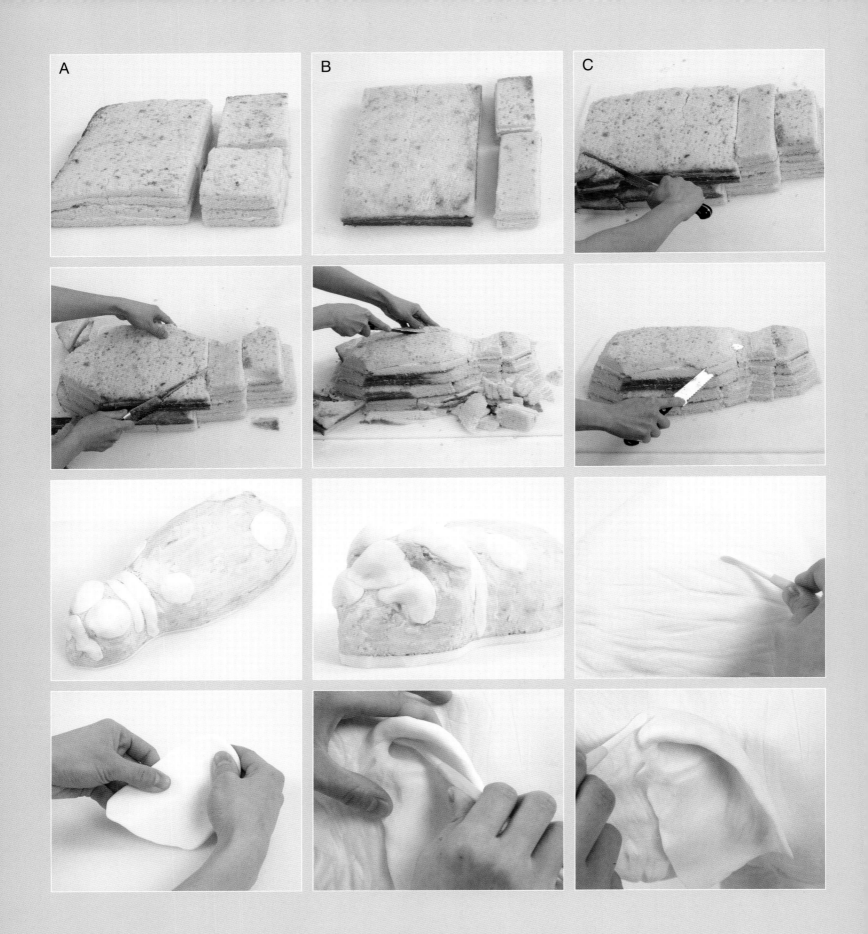

CARVING THE CAKE

15 Layer and fill both 30.5cm (12")
square cakes and trim off the crusts.
Cut each cake into three pieces, following
pictures A and B (opposite) as a guide.

16 Arrange the sections of cake
according to picture C: the body is
made up of two tiers of cake. Place the top tier
and bottom tier foamboards under each tier.
Start by trimming off all the corners to make
the body rounded, then carve into shape
using the foamboards as a guide. Trim the
cake along the back and across the top of the
head to make them dome shaped: the dome
of the back should be higher than the head.
Once you're happy with the shape, remove
the top tier and insert six plastic dowels into
the bottom layer (see page 18). Replace the
top tier and crumb-coat the cake.

17 Stick small pieces of sugarpaste over
the crumb-coated body to build up
the shape of the elephant before you cover
the cake. Make two 1cm (³/₈") thick sausages
and stick them across the top of the neck to
make folds of skin.

18 Attach two thick circles of sugarpaste
to the top of the head to make two
domes, then add more pieces of sugarpaste
at the base of the trunk. Stick a circle of
sugarpaste at each of the leg joints and leave
space for the eye sockets. At this stage, you
can use the sugarpaste to fill in any gaps
in the cake and correct the body shape if
necessary.

COVERING THE CAKE

19 Roll out 2kg (4lb 6½oz) of Bridal
White sugarpaste to approximately
6mm (⁵/₁₆") thick, and cover the whole body all
in one go (see page 17).

20 Use a ball tool to make indents for
the eye sockets, then texture the
body using the same technique as for the
stomach.

21 Spread royal icing across the top of the
main armature and sit the cake on top,
making sure it lines up perfectly with the legs
before you secure it firmly in place. Cover the
join between the body and the stomach with
pieces of Bridal White sugarpaste.

> ### TOP TIP
>
> Don't worry if the joint isn't completely
> hidden, as you can disguise it with the
> skin texture.

22 Texture the head, neck and rump
using the same technique as for the
stomach. You do not need to texture the back
as this will be covered with the rug.

EARS

23 To make the ears, take a small
amount of Bridal White sugarpaste
and model it into a large triangular shape that is
approximately 12.5cm x 7.5cm (5" x 3") in size.
Use your thumbs to shape the ear and thin the
edges. Measure the ear against the head to
make sure it is in proportion. Repeat to make a
second ear.

24 Position the ears towards the back
of the top of the head, then attach
them down the sides with a little cooled, boiled
water. Once attached, press the blunt end of a
Dresden tool into the top of the ear to make the
ear hole, then smooth over the join between the
head and ear with the same tool.

EYES

25 Colour a small piece of Bridal White
sugarpaste with Chestnut paste
food colour and roll a ball that is approximately
5mm (¼") in diameter. To make the eyes equal
in size, cut the ball in half with a small palette
knife, then roll each piece into an even smaller

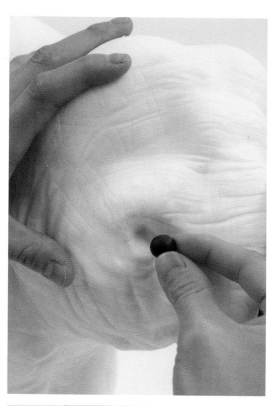

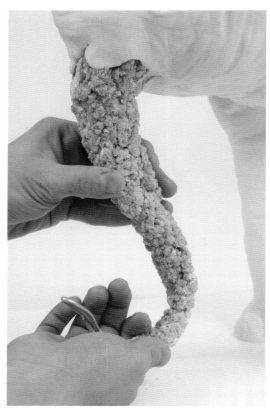

ball. Flatten the balls slightly and stick them into the eye sockets with a little cooled, boiled water.

TRUNK

26 In the same way as for the legs, build up the trunk around the wire armature with crisped rice cereal mix. Make the trunk thick at the top but gradually thinner as you move down towards the tip. When you are happy with the shape, spread a layer of royal icing over the whole trunk then cover it in a layer of pastillage in the same way as for the legs. Mark the nostrils in the end of the trunk with a ball tool.

TAIL

27 Roll out a sausage of pastillage that is approximately 2cm (¾") thick, then narrow it to 1cm (⅜") thick at one end. Cut to approximately 13cm (5") long, then make cuts into the thinner end of the tail with a Dresden tool to make the hair.

RUG AND CAP

28 Roll out 750g (1lb 10½oz) of Glamour Red sugarpaste to approximately 2mm (¹/₁₆") thick, then cut out a rectangle measuring 70cm x 25.5cm (27" x 10") in size. Dampen the back of the elephant with a little cooled, boiled water, then roll up the shorter ends of the rug until they meet in the middle. Place the paste onto the back and unroll the paste over each side, making sure the rug is central.

29 From the leftover Glamour Red sugarpaste, use a cutting wheel to cut out a triangle shape that is approximately 20cm x 15cm (8" x 6") in size. Dampen the top of the head with a little cooled, boiled water and stick the cap in place.

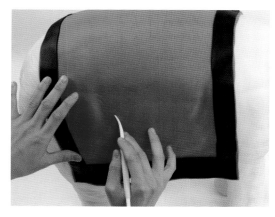

30 Roll out 250g (8¾oz) of Tuxedo Black sugarpaste very thinly and cut out several 3cm (1⅛") wide strips to make the border around the edge of the rug. Dampen the rug with a little cooled, boiled water and attach the strips approximately 3mm (⅛") in from the edge of the rug.

31 Following the picture of the elephant on pages 114–115 as a guide, use a Dresden tool to mark out the pattern on the sugarpaste while it is still soft.

32 Make up some soft-peak consistency royal icing and colour it with Jet Black paste food colour. Fit a piping bag with a no. 1 nozzle, fill the bag with the black icing and pipe on the black border design.

33 Make up some more royal icing and colour it with Poinsettia paste food colour. Following the marks you made earlier, use a no. 1 nozzle to pipe the design onto the red part of the rug.

PAINTING

34 Dust all the deep creases and folds (the ear holes, under the legs, behind the ears, under the eyes, the nostrils and toes) with Bulrush dust food colour and a flat paintbrush.

35 Mix six parts Marigold with one part Bulrush liquid food colour, then use the colour to airbrush over the deeper, folded areas under the belly, on the legs and under the neck. Airbrush just Marigold liquid colour over the rest of the elephant. If you don't own an airbrush, you can achieve the same effect by brushing Chestnut dust food colour over the elephant using a dry, flat dusting brush.

36 Mix some Antique Gold lustre dust with a little confectioners' glaze in a paint palette. Use a no. 1 paintbrush to paint over the piped pattern. Pipe some Poinsettia-coloured icing over the gold trim in a wavy pattern.

37 Brush confectioners' glaze over the eyes to make them shine. Clean the brush with glaze cleaner after use.

38 Trim the cake drum with gold satin ribbon to finish.

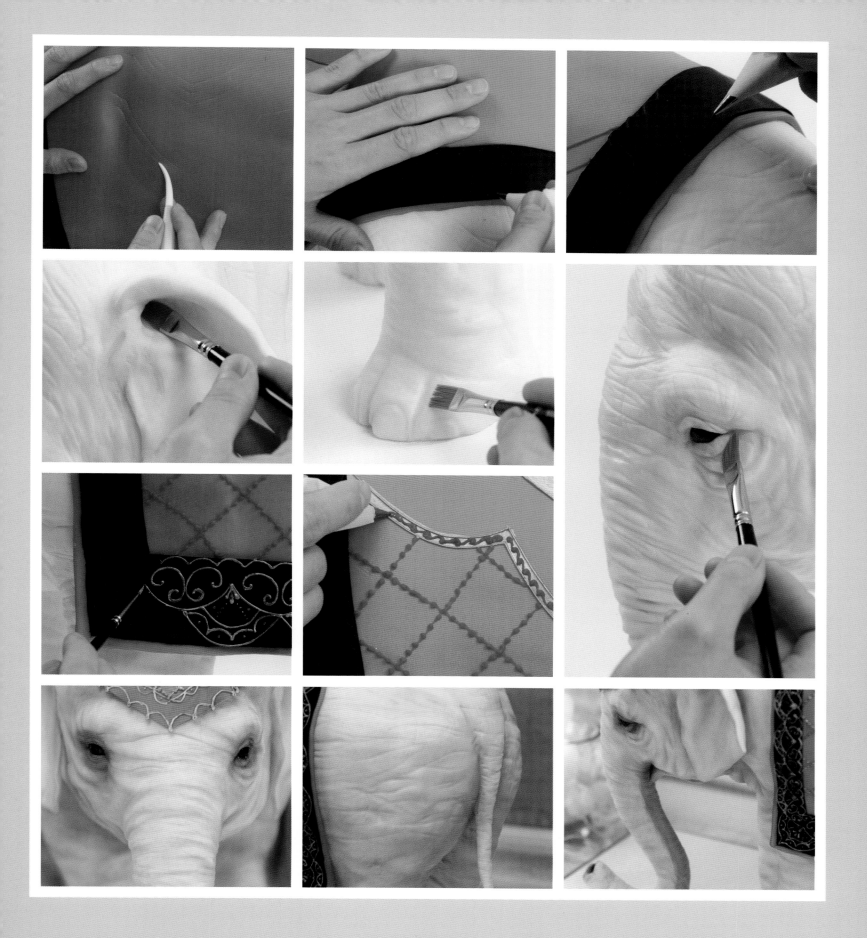

Indian Wedding
Elephant

SUMMER WEDDING GAZEBO

Perfect for a small outdoor wedding, this unique gazebo design is made from sponge cake. The design could be adapted to suit the wedding venue by changing the colour and style of the building.

Size: approx. 15cm x 15cm x 35.5cm (6" x 6" x 14") | Serves 25

EDIBLES

15.5cm and 20.5cm (6" x 8") square sponge cakes, layered and filled

1 quantity of buttercream (see page 12)

SK Sugarpaste (rolled fondant): 600g (1lb 5¼oz) Bridal White, 500g (1lb 1¾oz) Ruby Rose, 100g (3½oz) Coco Brown

Modelling paste (sugarpaste + CMC, see page 12): 60g (2oz) Palm Green

500g (1lb 1¾oz) SK Pastillage Powder

250g (8¾oz) SK Instant Mix Royal Icing

SK Professional Paste Food Colours: Bulrush (dark brown), Edelweiss (white), Holly/Ivy (dark green), Sunflower

SK Designer Metallic Lustre Dust Food Colour: Antique Gold

SK Confectioners' Glaze

SK Professional Liquid Food Colours (for airbrushing): Blackberry (black), Chestnut (soft beige), Marigold (tangerine)

Clear alcohol, e.g. vodka or gin

EQUIPMENT

Basic equipment (see pages 6–9)

25.5cm (10") round cake drum (board)

15cm and 20.5cm (6"and 8") square pieces of 5mm (¼") thick foamboard

6 plastic cake dowels

Miniature brickwork embosser (PC)

Round cutters: 2.2cm, 4cm (¾", 1½")

Piping nozzles: nos. 1, 50S

Clean food-grade sponge

New, clean scouring pads

Satin ribbon: 84cm (33") x 15mm (⅝") width white

Templates and diagrams (see pages 140–141)

CAKE BOARDS

1 Cover the cake drum with Bridal White sugarpaste (see page 16) and give it a stone texture following step 11 on page 99. Allow to dry.

2 Make a copy of the top and bottom tier board templates. Place the top tier template onto the 15cm (6") square foamboard and cut around it with a craft knife.

3 Place the bottom tier template onto the 20.5cm (8") foamboard and draw around it: this will be the board that you place the bottom tier on.

TOP TIP

I recommend that you make the gazebo at least one week in advance of serving the cake, as it needs to dry in several stages. The base of the gazebo, which is made from cake, could be made three days in advance so that it is fresh on the day.

GAZEBO STRUCTURE

4 Before you start, cut out all of the gazebo templates. Follow the instructions on the packet to make up the pastillage. Roll it out 1cm (3/8") thick, place the top tier board template onto the paste and cut around it with a cutting wheel to make the gazebo base. Make a hole in each corner of the base using a cocktail stick, following the template as a guide. Leave the base to dry on a spare cake board, turning it over after at least eight hours to allow the other side to dry.

5 Roll out some pastillage to a thickness of 1cm (3/8") and cut out eight posts using the template, a ruler and a cutting wheel. Insert a cocktail stick into one end of each post.

6 Roll out some pastillage to 3mm (1/8") thick and use the templates to cut out eight top beams, seven balustrade top railings, seven wider strips for the bottom balustrade

railings and eight rafters. Cut both ends of each rafter at a 45° angle as shown on the template.

7 Roll out another piece of pastillage to 2mm (1/16") thick and cut out 35 short balusters and eight fascia boards following the templates.

8 Make a copy of the roof section template. Mix 200g (7oz) of pastillage with Bulrush paste food colour and roll it out to approximately 2mm (1/16") thick. Use the brickwork embosser to impress a tile pattern evenly over the paste. Using the roof section template and a cutting wheel, cut out eight roof pieces from the embossed paste.

9 For the stairs, roll out some more pastillage to 3mm (1/8") thick and cut out three top rails, 10 side balusters and seven central balusters. Roll out some Bridal White sugarpaste to 2mm (1/16") thick and cut out 10 panels for the stepping stones.

10 Let all the pieces dry completely in a warm, dry atmosphere before assembly.

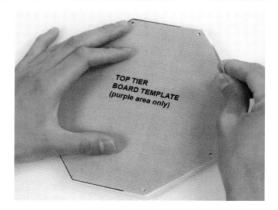

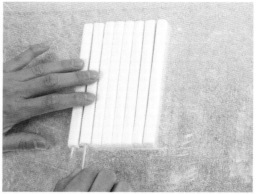

ASSEMBLING THE GAZEBO

TOP TIP

Always use royal icing to stick dried pieces of sugarpaste or pastillage together; use cooled, boiled water to stick soft sugarpaste to pastillage.

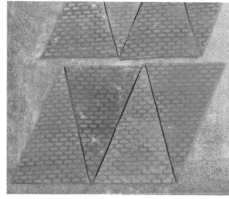

Balustrades

11 Lay out all the pieces for the balustrades flat on a spare cake board and stick five short balusters to each bottom railing: start with one railing in the middle, then stick two equally spaced strips on either side of the central railing. Stick one top railing across the top of the balusters. Repeat to make five more balustrades in the same way. Allow them to dry completely.

12 Stick the posts into each of the holes on the gazebo base. Attach a beam between the top of each post, then secure each of the balustrades to the base between the posts. There should be one section of the gazebo without a balustrade: this is the entrance at the front. Neaten the joins with a fine paintbrush then leave to dry.

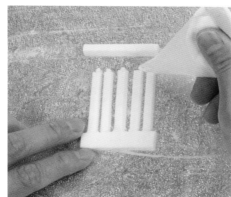

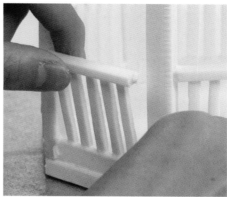

Roof

13 Roll a 1cm (³⁄₈") ball of pastillage and stick the angled end of two rafters to the ball on opposite sides. Attach the other end of the rafters to the top of the posts. Working with two rafters at a time, continue to stick sets of rafters around the central ball to create the framework for the roof. Leave it to dry completely.

14 Pipe a line of royal icing around the underside of a roof piece and attach it to the top of two rafters. Repeat with the remaining roof sections and allow to dry completely.

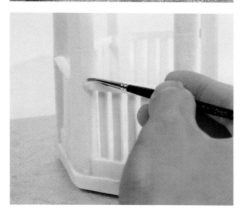

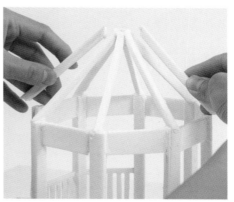

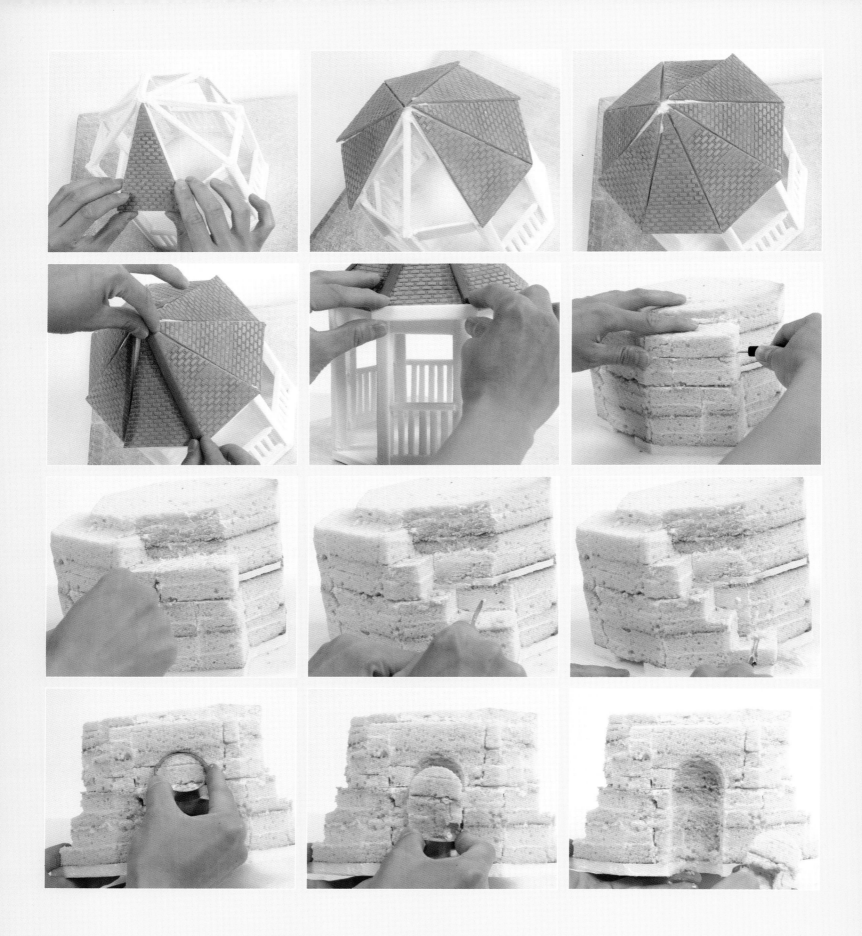

15 Colour some Bridal White sugarpaste with Bulrush paste food colour and roll it out very thinly. Cut out eight 5mm (¼") wide strips that are approximately 10cm (4") long. Attach each strip over the joint between the roof sections and trim to size if necessary.

16 Attach the fascia boards across the base of each roof section.

17 Roll out a small amount of Bridal White sugarpaste, cut out a small circle using a 2.2cm (¾") round cutter and stick it over the very top of the roof. Make a 1cm (³/₈") half-sphere from Bridal White sugarpaste and attach it on top of the circle. Model a pointed cone that is approximately 1cm (³/₈") tall and stick it on top of the half-sphere with the point sticking upwards.

CARVING THE CAKE

18 Place the top tier foamboard on the 15cm (6") square cake then use a serrated knife and carving diagram A on page 141 to carve the cake into a heptagonal shape. Keep the off-cuts from three corners of the cake.

19 Position the bottom tier foamboard on the 20.5cm (8") square cake then carve the cake into shape following diagram B on page 141. Keep the off-cuts that are numbered 4 and 5 on the diagram.

20 Place the foamboards underneath the cakes and insert three dowels into the bottom tier to support the tier above (see page 18). Place the smaller top tier on top, making sure the back of the cake is aligned with the bottom tier. Arrange the off-cuts around the front of the top tier cake following diagram C on page 141 to extend the top tier.

21 Carve the stairs into each side using a paring knife. Cut five equal sections, making each step approximately 1.5cm (½") in size.

22 Use a 4cm (1½") round cutter to cut away the front of the cake and make the archway. Start approximately 2.5cm (1") from the top of the cake and pull the cutter down to the bottom of the cake, flush with the foamboard.

COVERING THE CAKE

23 Position the cake centrally on the covered cake drum then crumb-coat the whole cake with buttercream (see page 14).

24 Mix together 500g (1lb 1¾oz) of Ruby Rose, 100g (3½oz) of Coco Brown and 100g (3½oz) of Bridal White sugarpaste to make a red brick colour. Knead the paste well until all the colours are evenly combined.

25 Roll out the brick-coloured sugarpaste to approximately 5mm (¼") thick and emboss the paste evenly with the brickwork embosser. Use the paste to cover the cake in sections, ensuring you line up the brickwork pattern neatly.

26 Roll out some Bridal White sugarpaste to approximately 5mm (¼") and use the paste to cover the stairs, the top of the cake and the inside of the archway in sections.

DECORATING THE GAZEBO

27 Roll out some Bridal White sugarpaste to approximately 1cm (³/₈") thick and cut out a long strip that is 1cm (³/₈") wide to make a white trim for the stairs. Attach it down the top of the stairs with a little cooled, boiled water.

28 Use royal icing to stick the stone steps to the top of each stair so they slightly overhang the edge.

29 Roll out some Bridal White sugarpaste very thinly and cut out long strips that are approximately 1cm (³/₈") wide. Attach the strips around the base of the cake with a little cooled, boiled water to make the wall plinth.

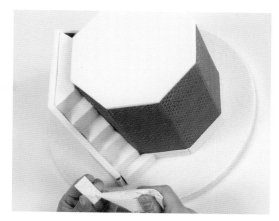

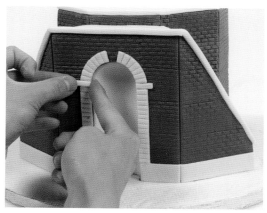
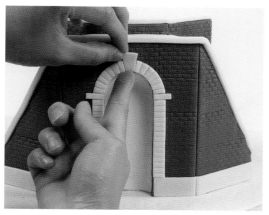

30   For the trim around the archway, cut out another 1cm (3/8") wide strip of thinly rolled Bridal White sugarpaste. Attach it around the edge of the arch and trim to size. Starting from the base of the archway, use the edge of a ruler to mark lines in 5mm (1/4") intervals all the way around the trim. Leave a gap either side of the arch where it starts to curve and one at the top for the larger, decorative stones.

31   Roll out some more Bridal White sugarpaste to the same thickness, cut out two white strips that are slightly wider than 5mm (1/4") and stick them in the gaps on either side of the arch.

32   Cut a larger piece of Bridal White sugarpaste that is approximately 2cm x 1.5cm (3/4" x 5/8") in size. Make it slightly narrower at one end to make the keystone at the top of the arch. Stick it in the middle and cut off the trim underneath.

33   For the knee wall at the front of the archway, roll out some Bridal White sugarpaste to approximately 7mm (5/16") thick and cut a strip the same width as the wall plinth. Bend the paste into a curve at the front of the base of the wall.

34   Insert three plastic dowels into the top tier to support the gazebo (see page 18). Secure the gazebo centrally on the top tier with royal icing and make sure that the entrance is aligned with the stairs.

35   To make the handrail, attach seven evenly spaced central balusters along the top of the stairs, then attach five side balusters down either side of the stairs. Attach three top rails across the top of the balustrades. To finish, roll four 1cm (3/8") balls of Bridal White sugarpaste and stick two at either side of the top of the handrail and one at each end.

36   For the topiary tree, make a cone from a piece of Palm Green sugarpaste measuring 8cm (3 1/8") tall and approximately 3cm (1 1/8") in diameter at the base. Use a craft knife to cut it into three sections and roll the two lower sections into balls, leaving the pointed cone shape at the top. Roll each section between new, clean scouring pads to add some texture. Leave them to dry.

37   Stack the sections on top of each other and stick them together with royal icing. Paint the tree with Holly/Ivy paste food colour and Holly/Ivy mixed with a little Edelweiss paste food colour. Leave it to dry then secure the tree inside the archway.

PAINTING

38   Dilute some Antique Gold lustre dust with confectioners' glaze and use a fine paintbrush to paint the decoration on top of the gazebo.

39   Paint random sections of the brick walls with Bulrush paste food colour to add a realistic depth of colour. Spray the walls lightly using an airbrush and Chestnut liquid food colour.

40   Mix one part Blackberry liquid colour to eight parts clear alcohol to achieve grey, then use this to airbrush the stone base and the stairs.

41   Spray some of the stones on the board with Marigold liquid food colour using an airbrush, then paint the board with Bulrush paste food colour.

42   Colour some royal icing with Bulrush paste food colour. Fit a piping bag with a no. 1 nozzle and pipe some crawling ivy stems over the wall with the dark brown royal icing.

43   Colour some more royal icing with Holly/Ivy paste food colour. Fit a piping bag with a no. 50S nozzle and pipe small ivy leaves over the wall, around the entrance to the gazebo and in garlands around the posts.

44   For the tiny flowers, colour some royal icing with a little Sunflower paste food colour and pipe yellow and white leaf-shaped blossoms with a no. 1 nozzle between the leaves around the gazebo.

45   To finish, trim the cake board with white ribbon.

Summer Wedding
Gazebo

TEMPLATES

CLASSIC CAR
pages 24–33

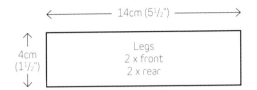

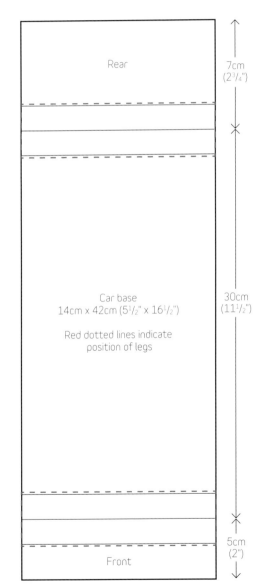

Legs
2 x front
2 x rear

4cm
(1½")

14cm (5½")

Rear

7cm
(2¾")

Car base
14cm x 42cm (5½" x 16½")

Red dotted lines indicate
position of legs

30cm
(11½")

5cm
(2")

Front

CAR ARMATURE DIAGRAM

SIDE PROFILE (LEFT)

Template at 50%. Enlarge to
200% for actual size

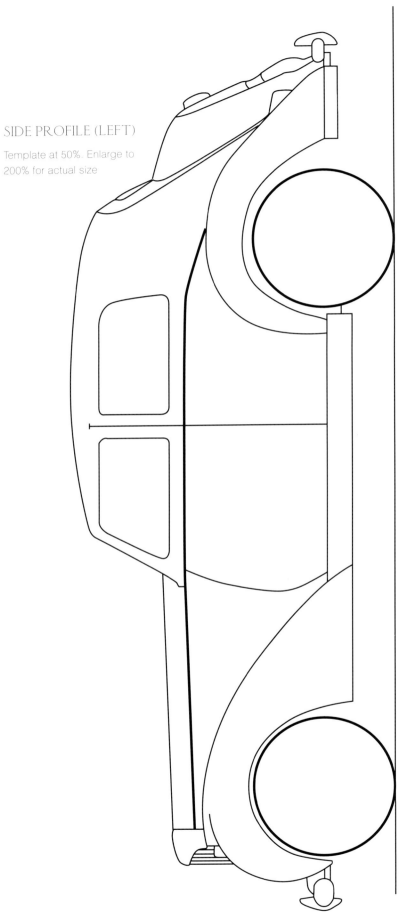

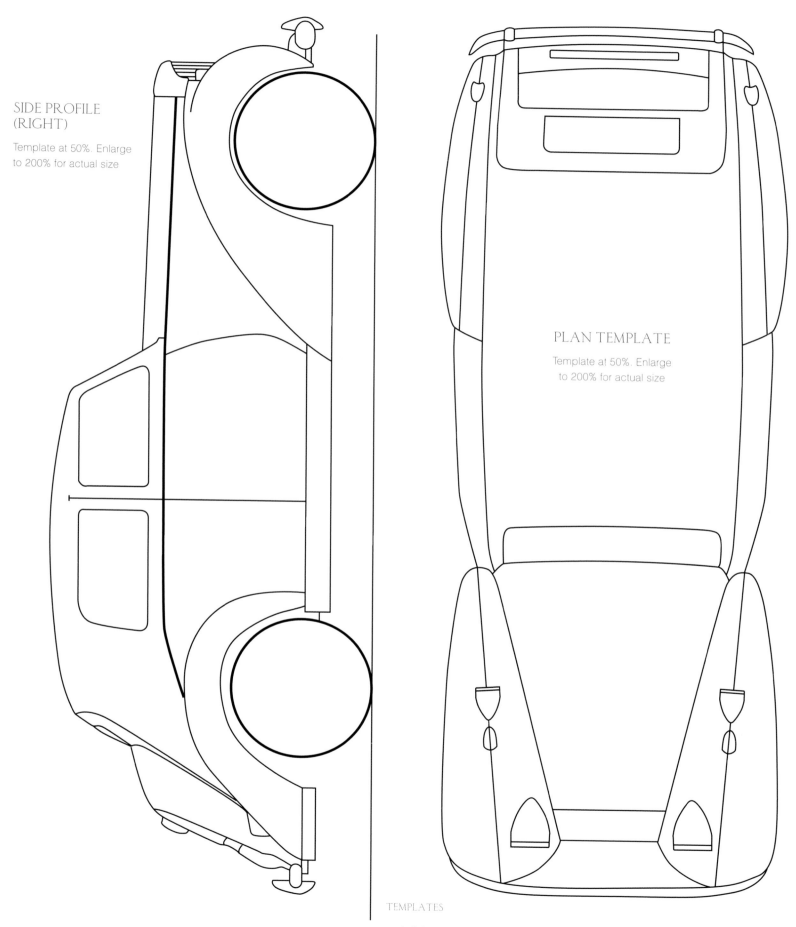

SIDE PROFILE
(RIGHT)

Template at 50%. Enlarge
to 200% for actual size

PLAN TEMPLATE

Template at 50%. Enlarge
to 200% for actual size

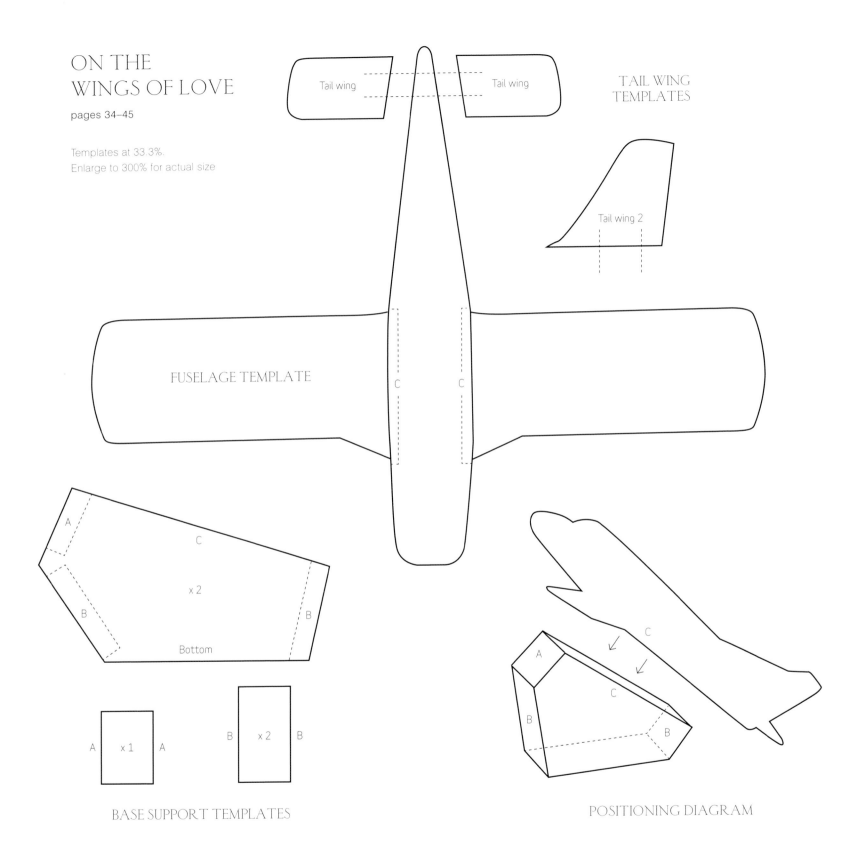

ON THE
WINGS OF LOVE

pages 34–45

Templates at 33.3%.
Enlarge to 300% for actual size

Tail wing

Tail wing

TAIL WING
TEMPLATES

Tail wing 2

FUSELAGE TEMPLATE

C   C

A

C

x 2

B   B

Bottom

A   x 1   A

B   x 2   B

BASE SUPPORT TEMPLATES

A

C

C

B

B

POSITIONING DIAGRAM

SOMETHING OLD, SOMETHING NEW

pages 46–56

Templates actual size

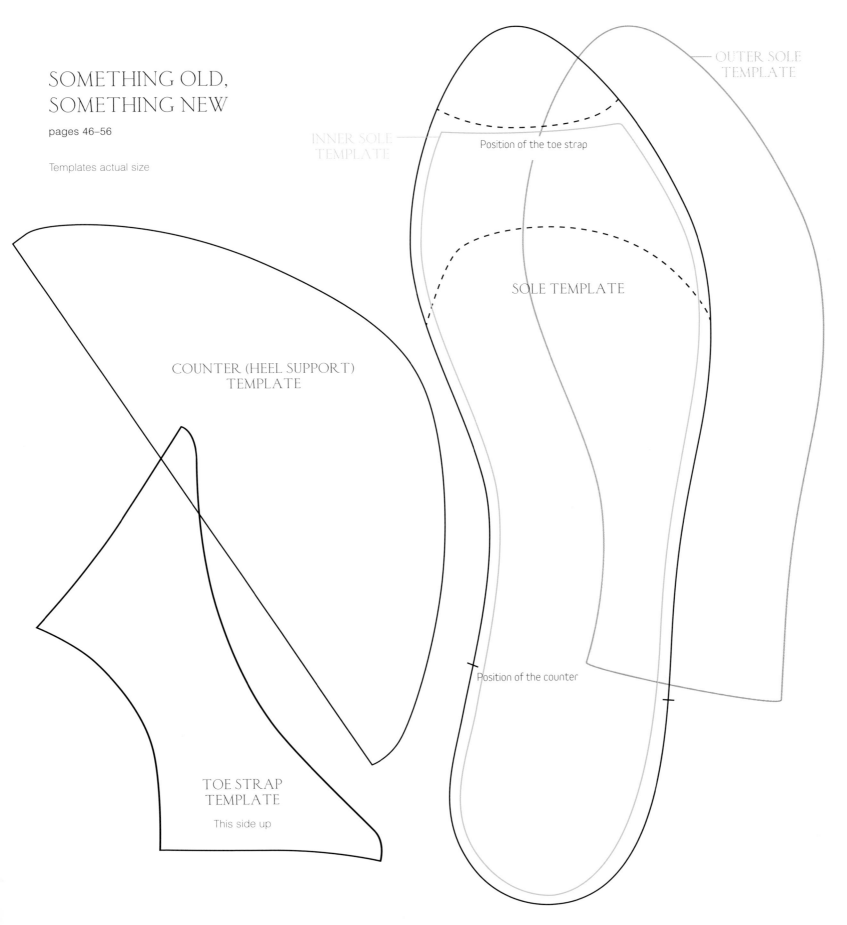

OUTER SOLE
TEMPLATE

INNER SOLE
TEMPLATE

Position of the toe strap

SOLE TEMPLATE

COUNTER (HEEL SUPPORT)
TEMPLATE

Position of the counter

TOE STRAP
TEMPLATE

This side up

ST BRIDE'S CHURCH
pages 56–65

DIAGRAM 1

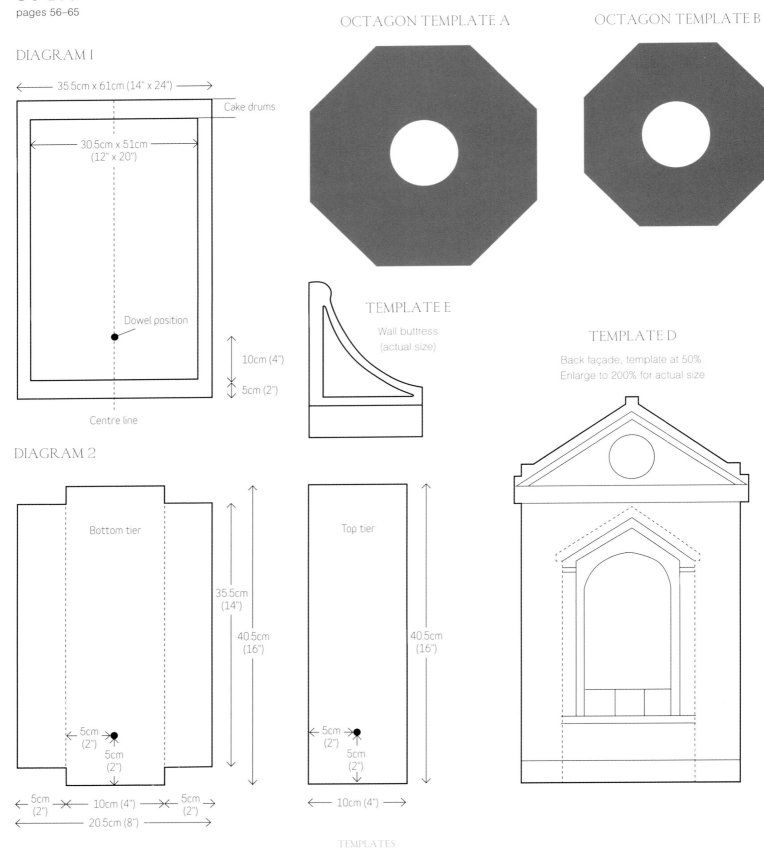

35.5cm x 61cm (14" x 24")

Cake drums

30.5cm x 51cm
(12" x 20")

Dowel position

10cm (4")

5cm (2")

Centre line

OCTAGON TEMPLATE A

OCTAGON TEMPLATE B

TEMPLATE E

Wall buttress
(actual size)

TEMPLATE D

Back façade, template at 50%.
Enlarge to 200% for actual size

DIAGRAM 2

Bottom tier

Top tier

35.5cm
(14")

40.5cm
(16")

40.5cm
(16")

5cm
(2")

5cm
(2")

5cm
(2")

5cm
(2")

5cm
(2")

10cm (4")

5cm
(2")

20.5cm (8")

10cm (4")

SPIRE TEMPLATE A

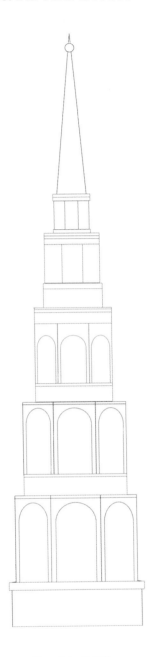

Template at 50%.
Enlarge to 200% for actual size

TEMPLATE C1

Arch window
(shaded area, actual size)

TEMPLATE C3

Tower window
(shaded area, actual size)

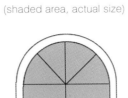

TEMPLATE C2

Back window
(shaded area, actual size)

TOWER TEMPLATE B

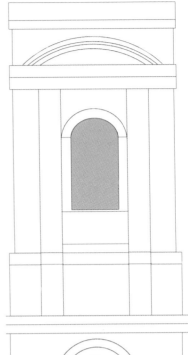

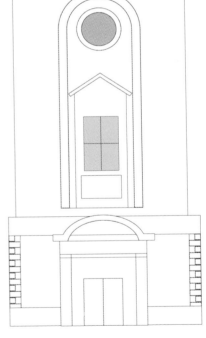

Template at 50%.
Enlarge to 200% for actual size

FIRST LOVE
pages 66–75

CUTTING THE CAKE

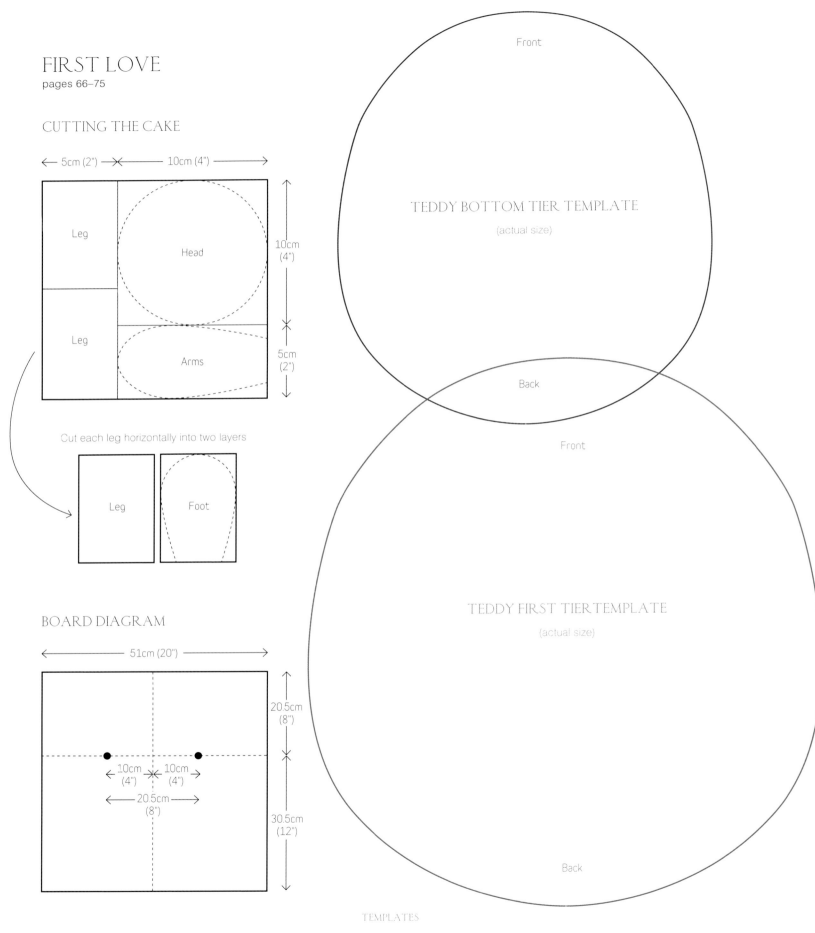

← 5cm (2") → ← 10cm (4") →

Leg

Head

10cm (4")

Leg

Arms

5cm (2")

Cut each leg horizontally into two layers

Leg

Foot

BOARD DIAGRAM

← 51cm (20") →

20.5cm (8")

← 10cm (4") → ← 10cm (4") →

← 20.5cm (8") →

30.5cm (12")

TEDDY BOTTOM TIER TEMPLATE

(actual size)

Front

Back

Front

TEDDY FIRST TIER TEMPLATE

(actual size)

Back

Front

HEAD TEMPLATE

(actual size)

Back

GROOM'S JACKET TEMPLATE

(actual size)

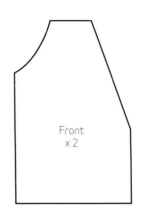

Front
x 2

Back

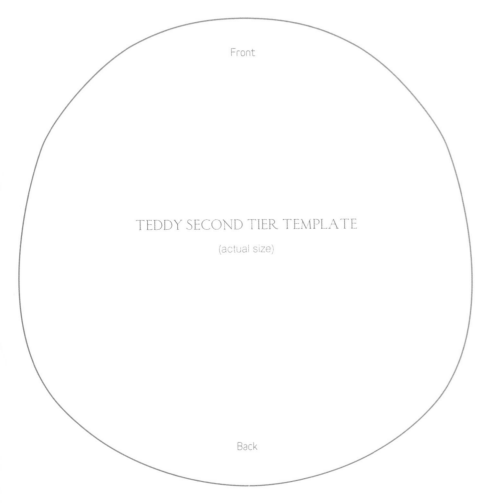

Front

TEDDY SECOND TIER TEMPLATE

(actual size)

Back

SWEETHEART SWANS
pages 76–85

ARMATURE DIAGRAM

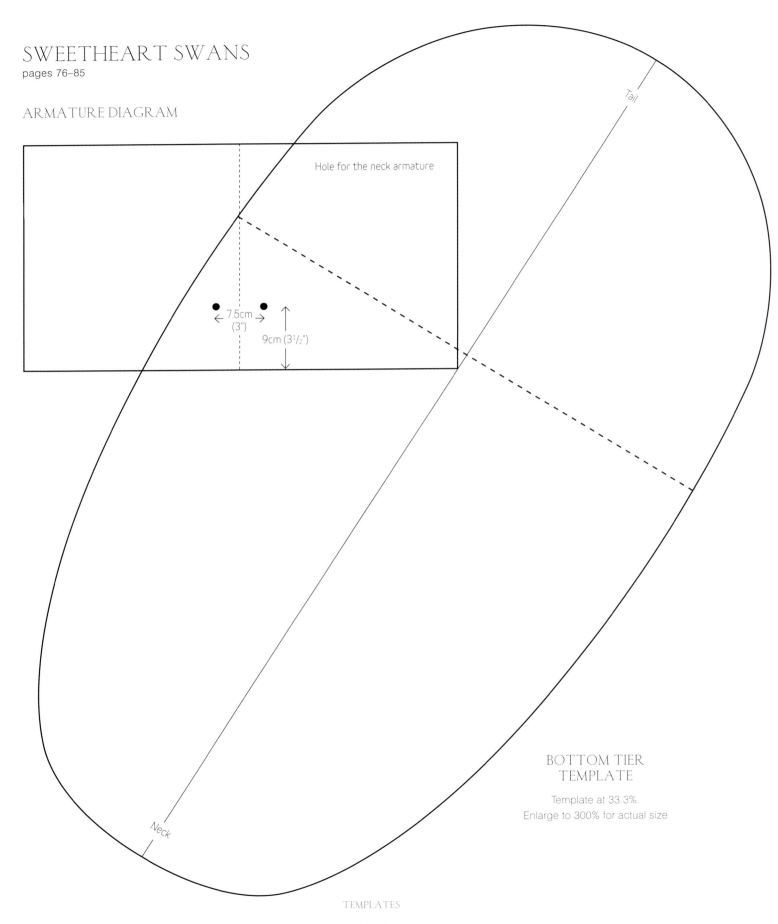

Hole for the neck armature

← 7.5cm →
(3")

9cm (3½")

Tail

Neck

BOTTOM TIER
TEMPLATE

Template at 33.3%.
Enlarge to 300% for actual size

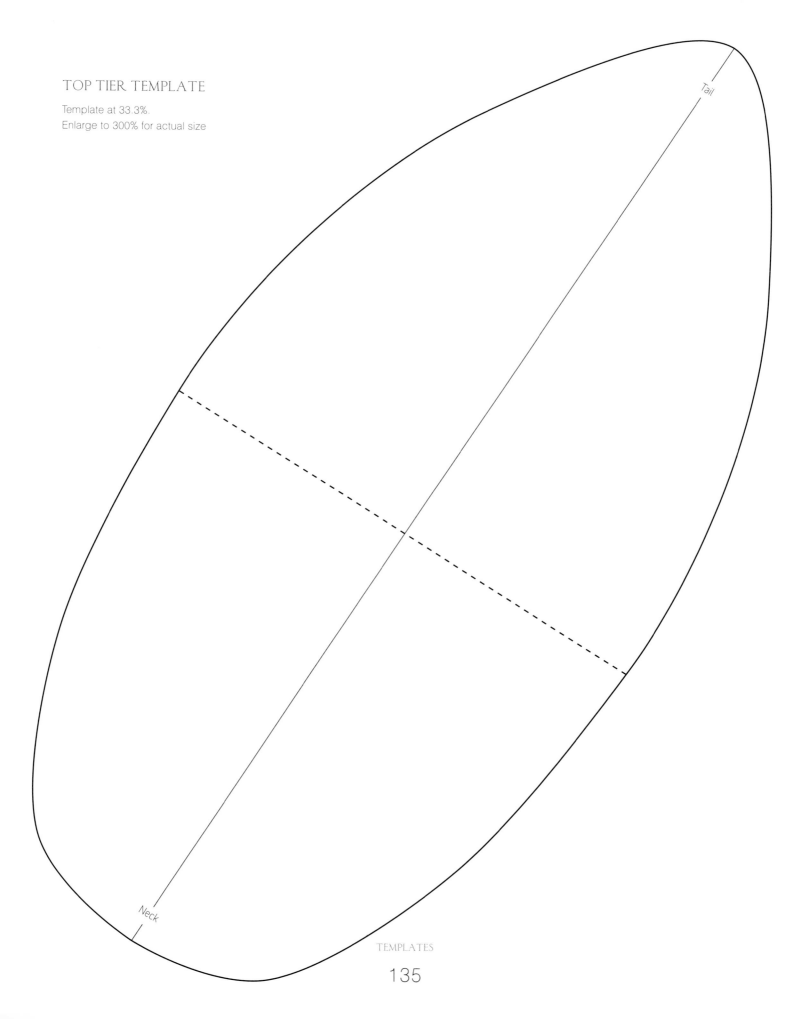

TOP TIER TEMPLATE

Template at 33.3%.
Enlarge to 300% for actual size

Tail

Neck

FOUNTAIN OF ETERNAL LOVE

pages 96–105

TOP PILLAR
TEMPLATE

(actual size)

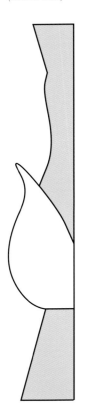

BOTTOM PILLAR
TEMPLATE

(actual size)

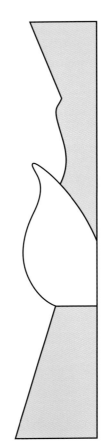

VASE TEMPLATE

(actual size)

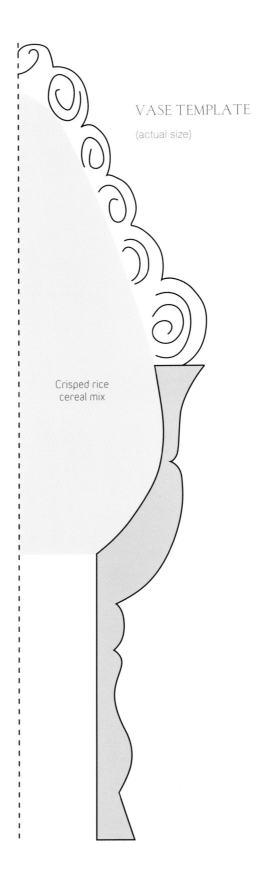

Crisped rice
cereal mix

INDIAN WEDDING ELEPHANT

pages 106–115

DIAGRAM 1

Positioning the leg armatures on the cake drum.

Draw an imaginary line diagonally from corner to corner. Position the back right leg on this line 18cm (7") from one corner and the back left leg directly above. The two front legs should sit either side of the line further up the board.

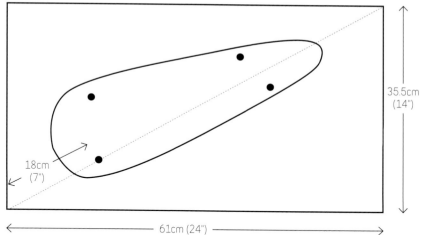

35.5cm (14")

61cm (24")

18cm (7")

DIAGRAM 2

Cutting the square cakes

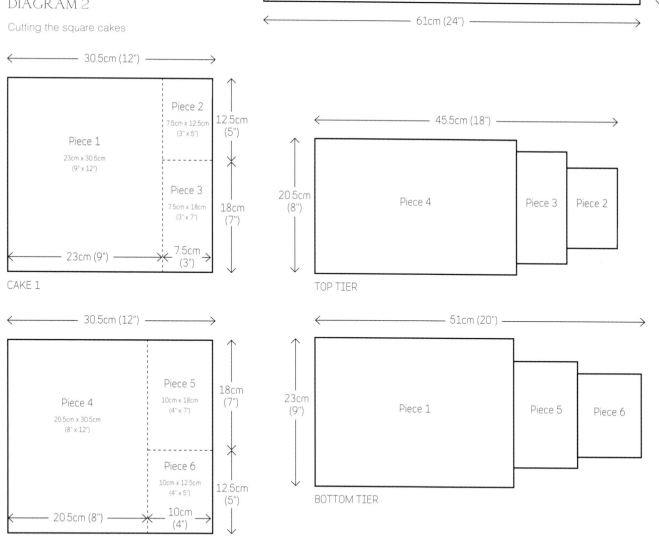

30.5cm (12")

Piece 2
7.5cm x 12.5cm
(3" x 5")

Piece 1
23cm x 30.5cm
(9" x 12")

Piece 3
7.5cm x 18cm
(3" x 7")

12.5cm (5")

18cm (7")

23cm (9")

7.5cm (3")

CAKE 1

45.5cm (18")

20.5cm (8")

Piece 4

Piece 3

Piece 2

TOP TIER

30.5cm (12")

Piece 5
10cm x 18cm
(4" x 7")

Piece 4
20.5cm x 30.5cm
(8" x 12")

Piece 6
10cm x 12.5cm
(4" x 5")

18cm (7")

12.5cm (5")

20.5cm (8")

10cm (4")

CAKE 2

51cm (20")

23cm (9")

Piece 1

Piece 5

Piece 6

BOTTOM TIER

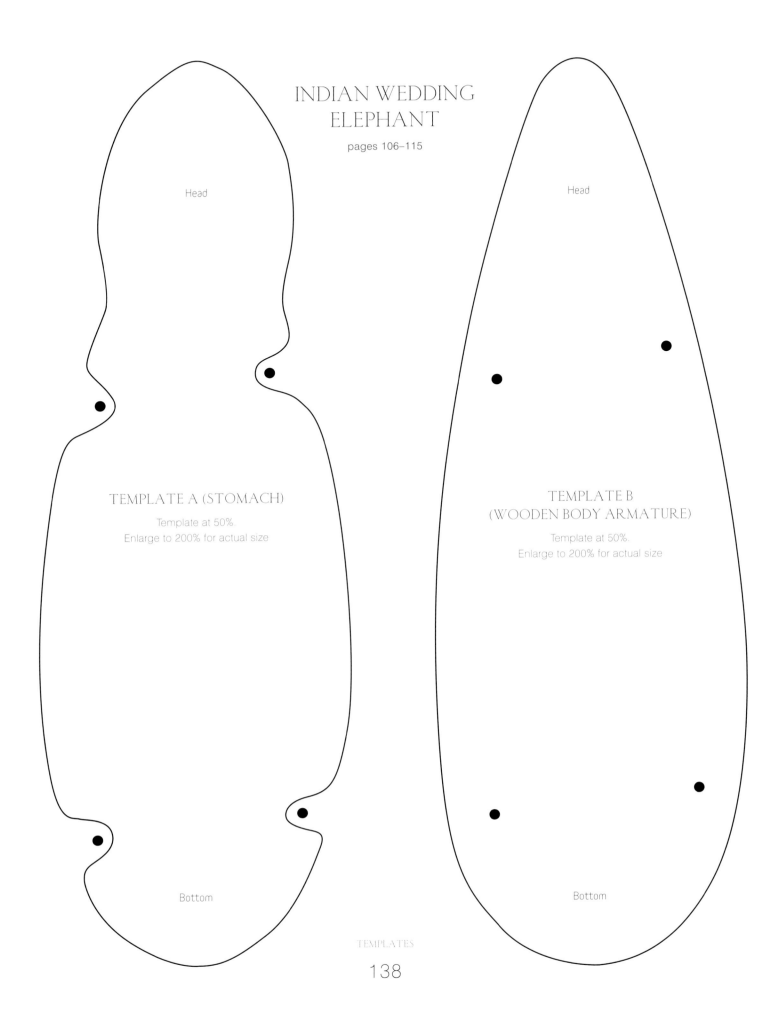

INDIAN WEDDING
ELEPHANT
pages 106–115

Head

Head

TEMPLATE A (STOMACH)

Template at 50%.
Enlarge to 200% for actual size

TEMPLATE B
(WOODEN BODY ARMATURE)

Template at 50%.
Enlarge to 200% for actual size

Bottom

Bottom

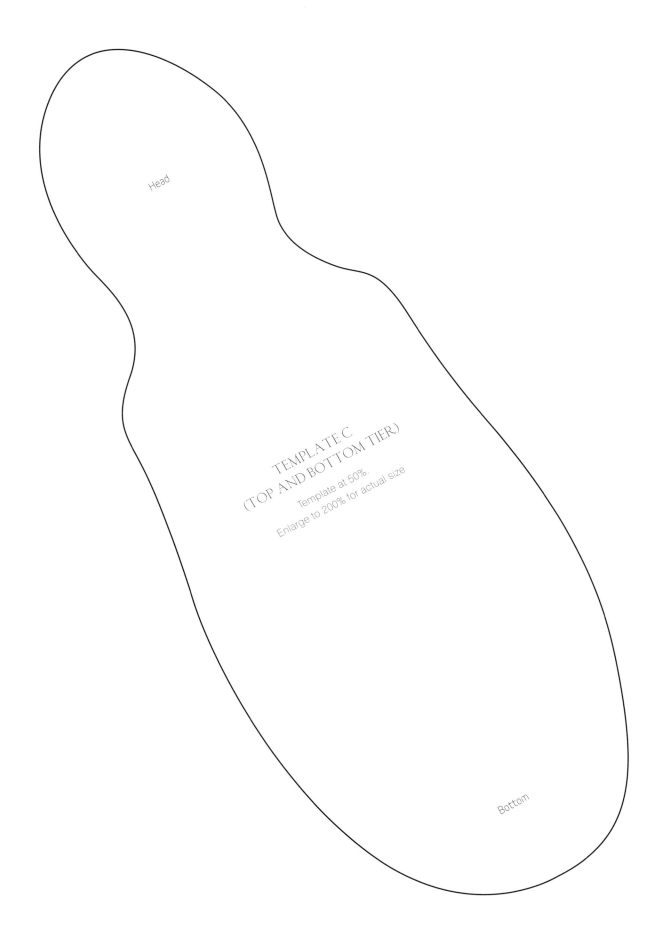

Head

TEMPLATE C
(TOP AND BOTTOM TIER)

Template at 50%.
Enlarge to 200% for actual size

Bottom

SUMMER WEDDING GAZEBO

pages 116–125

GAZEBO PIECES

(actual size)

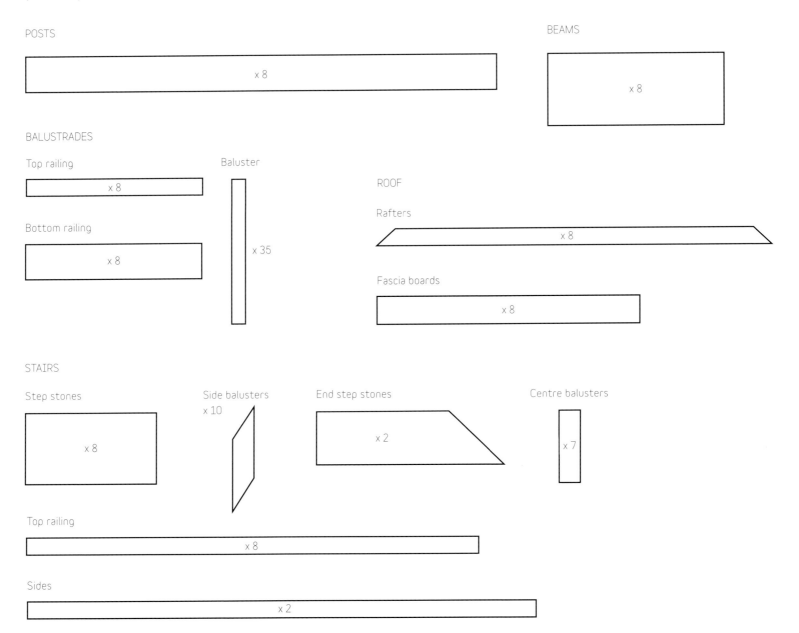

POSTS

x 8

BEAMS

x 8

BALUSTRADES

Top railing
x 8

Baluster
x 35

Bottom railing
x 8

ROOF

Rafters
x 8

Fascia boards
x 8

STAIRS

Step stones
x 8

Side balusters
x 10

End step stones
x 2

Centre balusters
x 7

Top railing
x 8

Sides
x 2

ROOF SHEET TEMPLATE

(actual size)

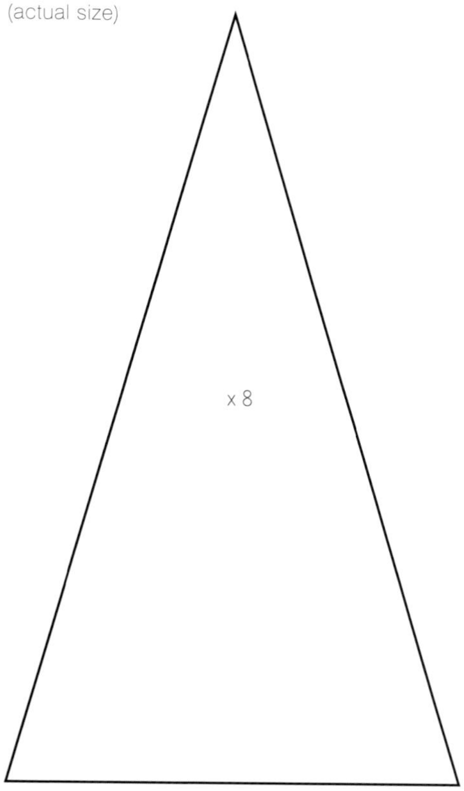

x 8

GAZEBO BOARD TEMPLATES

Template at 50%. Enlarge to 200% for actual size

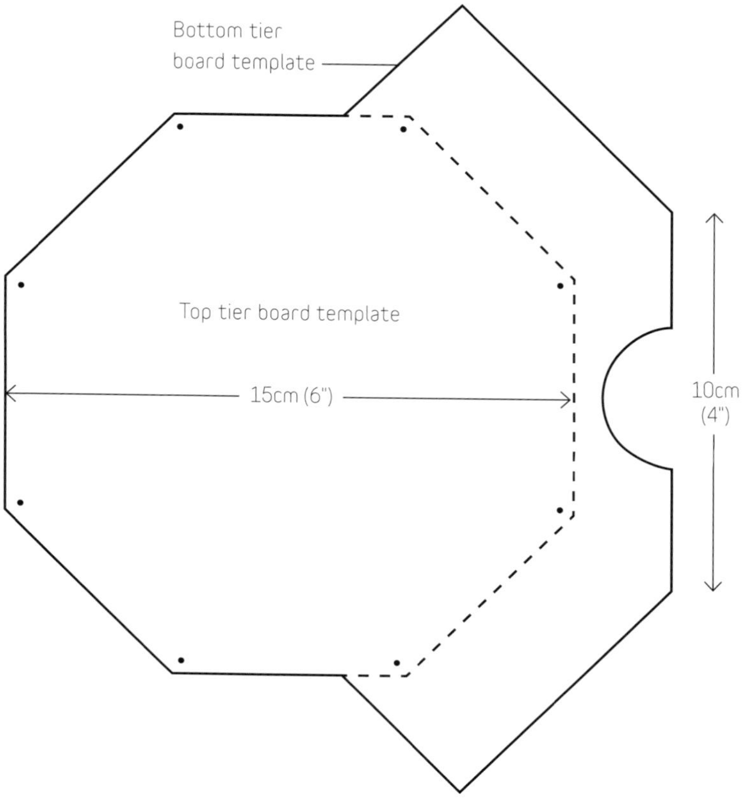

Bottom tier
board template

Top tier board template

15cm (6")

10cm
(4")

CARVING DIAGRAM

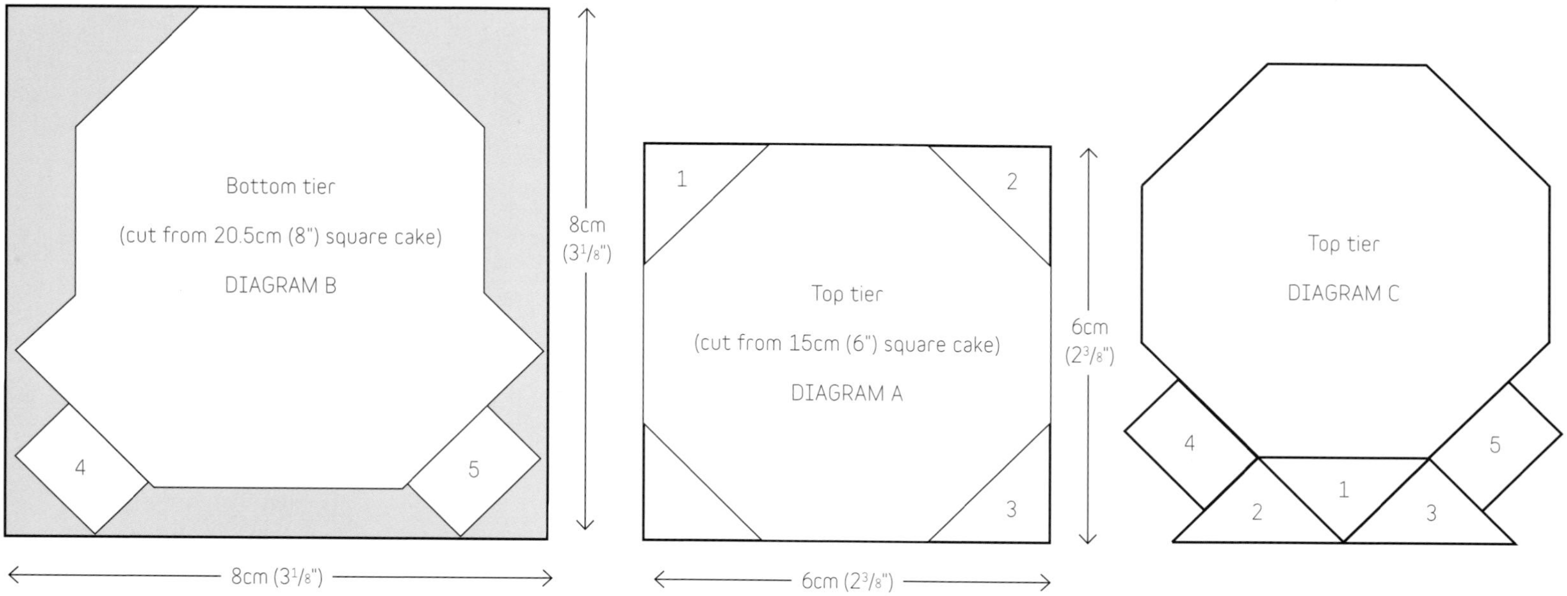

Bottom tier

(cut from 20.5cm (8") square cake)

DIAGRAM B

4

5

8cm
(3¹/₈")

8cm (3¹/₈")

1

2

Top tier

(cut from 15cm (6") square cake)

DIAGRAM A

3

6cm
(2³/₈")

6cm (2³/₈")

Top tier

DIAGRAM C

4

5

2

1

3

SUGAR ART GALLERY

Over the next few pages is a small selection of the extraordinary cake sculptures that Michelle has created for competitions, PR stunts, corporate events and exhibitions, as well as private commissions.

QUEEN ELIZABETH II AND WELSH CORGI
Michelle's lifelike cake sculptures of Queen Elizabeth II and a corgi, inspired by the Diamond Jubilee, won her Gold and Silver medals at the Culinary Olympics in 2012.

THE PEGASUS

Michelle was awarded a gold medal for her
22-inch tall sugar sculpture of Pegasus, at
Hotelympia Salon Culinaire 2008 in London.

STONE LECTERN CAKE

Michelle re-created the shape of a stone lectern in cake to celebrate the 150th anniversary of St John the Evangelist's Church in Burgess Hill, West Sussex.

REALISTIC BABY: Made from fruit cake, marzipan and sugarpaste, Michelle was invited to display this life-sized replica of a baby at the Victoria & Albert Museum, London.

SUCKLING PIG CAKE: Michelle displayed this realistic suckling pig cake at the Experimental Food Society 'Spectacular' event in 2010 where it was served as part of an eight-course banquet.

GIANT CAKE SCULPTURE OF A COW: Weighing in at approximately 120kg, it would take five people to safely transport this anatomically correct, near life-size cow cake. This sculpture was privately commissioned for a wedding.

'MUNCHY' THE JACK RUSSELL: Well-known for her realistic animal creations, Michelle teaches students all over the world how to make this 16-inch tall Jack Russell dog on one of her classes.

3D BRONZE-EFFECT HORSE'S HEAD: This majestic 2ft tall horse head sculpture is made entirely from layered sponge cake, which Michelle covered with sugarpaste then textured and coloured to create the bronzed effect.

HOUND DOG: Inspired by the famous Elvis song, Michelle won Gold at the 2008 Culinary Olympics
with this edible hound dog which took 45 hours to make and weighs 20kg.

PIRATE SKULL CAKE: This life-size skull is carved from cake and the dagger, coins and treasure map are all made from sugar.

HALLOWEEN BIRTHDAY CAKE:

This life-size skull and pumpkin are carved from cake and decorated with sugar.

happy birthday Sirina

LONDON WEST END SPONGESCRAPER

This bird's eye view of London's West End was commissioned to celebrate 1,415 birthday years being marked by over 15 well-known local retailers.

QUEEN ELIZABETH II

LEFT: IMPERIAL WEST ARCHITECTURE CAKE

This edible architectural model for Imperial College London took 80 hours to make and used 30kg of sugarpaste.

T. REX CAKE SCULPTURE:

This 20-inch tall 3D cake sculpture of a Tyrannosaurus Rex needed a more advanced armature to ensure that the dinosaur remained in position.

Squires Kitchen, UK
3 Waverley Lane
Farnham
Surrey
GU9 8BB
0845 61 71 810
+44 (0) 1252 260 260
www.squires-shop.com

Squires Kitchen International School
The Grange
Hones Yard
Farnham
Surrey
GU9 8BB
0845 61 71 810
+44 (0) 1252 260 260
www.squires-school.co.uk

Squires Kitchen, France
+33 (0) 1 82 88 01 66
clientele@squires-shop.fr
www.squires-shop.fr

Squires Kitchen, Spain
+34 93 180 7382
cliente@squires-shop.es
www.squires-shop.es

Squires Kitchen, Italy
cliente@squires-shop.it
www.squires-shop.it

Squires Kitchen, Germany
kunde@squires-shop.de
www.squires-shop.de

Distributors

UK
Culpitt Ltd.
Northumberland
www.culpitt.com

Guy, Paul & Co. Ltd.
Buckinghamshire
www.guypaul.co.uk

Squires Kitchen
Surrey
www.squires-shop.com

For your nearest sugarcraft supplier, please contact your local distributor.

Europe
Cake Supplies
Netherlands
www.cakesupplies.nl

Dom Konditera LLC
Belarus
www.domkonditera.com

Sugar World – Aliprantis Ltd.
Greece
www.sugarworld.gr

Tårtdecor
Küngalv
www.tartdecor.se